WHAT'S THE NUMBER FOR 911 AGAIN?

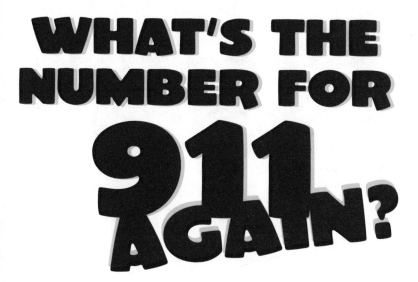

WHAT'S THE NUMBER FOR 911 AGAIN?

Leland Gregory

**Andrews McMeel
Publishing**

Kansas City

01 02 03 04 05 RDC 10 9 8 7 6 5 4 3 2 1

ISBN: 0-7407-1857-6

Library of Congress Catalog Card Number: 2001086444

Book design by Holly Camerlinck

THIS BOOK IS DEDICATED TO MY WIFE,
GLORIA GRAVES GREGORY.
SHE'S ALL I EVER WANTED AND
MORE THAN I DESERVE.

ACKNOWLEDGMENTS

I would like to acknowledge the following men and women who not only provided me with stories of stupid 911 phone calls but who also dedicated their lives to helping others. They are all kind, intelligent, and funny people and I'm honored to know them. Thank you.

Dawn Albert	Valerie Oberly
Kathy Alvarez	Linda Olmstead
Dave Bridgewaters	Peggy O'Rourke
John Burruss	Stacy Owens
Sandi Dawson	Jon H. Ronan
JoAnn Dixon	Amy Ross
Anneliese Edington	Ron Seguin
Laurie Frederickson	Charles Shinn
Lyle Gensler	Stephanie Subia
Pam Guadan	Holly Tran
Steve Heisinger	Michael R. Weston
Sonia Kelly	John Yeast

I want to send a very special "Thank You!" to Cheryl Valle and Kim Winward. They helped me uncover stories and transcripts, gave me advice and contacts, and went out of their way to make this book better and funnier than the first. Cheryl has been instrumental in helping my efforts become more acceptable and appreciated in the 911 community. Kim supplied me with numerous stories and, in addition to being a full-time dispatcher, is leading the fight for greater awareness of Spinal Muscular Atrophy. Please visit her site at: www.our-sma-angels.com/myheros.

I can't thank either of you enough.

AN EVERYDAY OCCURRENCE

DISPATCHER: Emergency.

MAN: Oh, I'm sorry. I thought I dialed Information.

DISPATCHER: No, sir. That would be 411.

THIS EARTHQUAKE
HAS BEEN SCHEDULED
FOR YOUR CONVENIENCE

During the Loma Prieta earthquake of October 17, 1989, a male called the communications center time and time again asking the same question: "When will the next aftershock be?" The caller was told repeatedly not to tie up the emergency line with questions that couldn't possibly be answered. He became more and more impatient with each call of "When will the next aftershock be?" until finally one fed-up dispatcher responded, "We've scheduled one for about five minutes from now; hang on!"

WHAT'S THE NUMBER FOR 911 AGAIN?

THE TV'S OKAY—
BUT YOU'RE BUSTED

MAN: Yeah, hi, is this 911?

DISPATCHER: Yes it is.

MAN: Yeah, listen now. If someone comes into my
              house, uh my fiancée, okay, and takes my
              TV and sells it while I went out to get her some
              rolled tacos, now, can you get her busted
              for that?

DISPATCHER: What city are you talking about, sir?

MAN: She took my TV and sold it out of my house.

DISPATCHER: Okay, let me get you the police department.

FREE WILLY

DISPATCHER: 911 emergency.

MAN: This is something you've got to see. This is unbelievable.

DISPATCHER: The Scottish Inn.

MAN: Yes.

DISPATCHER: And what's the problem there?

MAN: I got a man stuck in the pool. He's got his privates stuck in the pump line.

DISPATCHER: What? You're kidding me.

MAN: I'm telling you, honest to God, this is something you really got to see to believe.

DISPATCHER: North Florida?

MAN: Yes, ma'am.

DISPATCHER: 244 (laugh). You gotta stop laughing.

MAN: Yeah, this is something you don't see every day now.

DISPATCHER: And he's in the pool.

MAN: He's in the pool. He's been in there for three hours [laugh]. It's got to be shriveled up like hell, I guess. I'm sorry.

DISPATCHER: You can't keep doing this. Okay, are you security there?

MAN: Yeah, but I'm the night clerk here.

DISPATCHER: You're the night clerk [laughter]. You can't keep laughing.

REPEAT OFFENDER

It was a mystery that even the ingenious Mrs. Marple couldn't figure out. Why was someone repeatedly dialing 911 without speaking to the dispatcher? It could possibly be a silent cry for help—someone in real trouble who was unable to speak. When Boynton Beach, Florida, police rushed to the apartment of Barbara Marple, they solved the riddle for the recurring rings. Barbara, a twenty-three-year-old supermarket employee, denied making the calls. After some deductive reasoning the detectives quickly surmised who the culprit was. It wasn't Ms. Marple and it wasn't the butler (there wasn't one this time). It was Kitten! Not a bleach-blond bimbo, but a calico cat named Kitten. Police discovered the cat in the bedroom with its paw on the redial button. But the phone wasn't programmed to dial 911. The cat had pawed out *9*, then *1*, then another *1*— and then continued hitting the redial button. The kitty culprit was collared and later cuddled by Ms. Marple, whose only explanation of the cat's activity was, "She was probably trying to call my mother in New Jersey." Hmm, a likely story!

-- 911 REPORT --

"I left my car in a ditch and I'm now at home.
Can I get an officer to stop by my car and grab the
presents I left in it and bring them to me?"

DEDUCTIVE REASONING

LITTLE GIRL: Yeah, I need some help.

DISPATCHER: What's the matter?

LITTLE GIRL: With my math.

DISPATCHER: With your mouth?

LITTLE GIRL: No, with my math. I have to do it. Will you help me?

DISPATCHER: Sure, where do you live?

LITTLE GIRL: No, with my math.

DISPATCHER: Yeah, I know it. Where do you live, though?

LITTLE GIRL: No. I want you to talk with me on the phone.

DISPATCHER: No, I can't do that. I can send someone out to help you.

LITTLE GIRL: Okay. Um.

DISPATCHER: What kind of math do you have that you need help with?

LITTLE GIRL: I have, I have take-aways.

DISPATCHER: Oh, you gotta do the take-aways?

LITTLE GIRL: Yeah.

DISPATCHER: All right, what's the problem?

LITTLE GIRL: Um? You have to help me with my math.

DISPATCHER: Okay, tell me what the math is.

LITTLE GIRL: Okay, sixteen . . .

DISPATCHER: Yeah?

LITTLE GIRL: . . . take away eight.

DISPATCHER: Uh-huh.

LITTLE GIRL: Is what?

DISPATCHER: You tell me. How much do you think it is?

LITTLE GIRL: I don't know—one?

DISPATCHER: No. How old are you?

LITTLE GIRL: I'm only four!

DISPATCHER: Four?!

LITTLE GIRL: Yeah.

DISPATCHER: Yeah. What's another problem? That was a tough one.

LITTLE GIRL: Um. Oh, here's one. Five take away five.

DISPATCHER: Five take away five. And how much do you think that is?

LITTLE GIRL: Five?

MOTHER: Charleen, what are you doing?!

LITTLE GIRL: This policeman is helping me with my math.

MOTHER: What did I tell you about playing on the phone?

DISPATCHER: [to someone] It's probably her mother.

LITTLE GIRL: You said when I need help to call somebody.

MOTHER: I didn't mean the police!

YOU GOTTA HAND IT TO HIM

Michael Murray's hand was so damaged he knew he needed help—so he called 911. When the paramedics and the police arrived at his apartment in Albany, New York, they were a little suspicious of Murray's explanation of his hurt hand. He claimed he had cut it mowing the lawn. The only problem with his story was that it was during the April Fool's Day snowstorm of 1997—and the guy lived in an apartment. After a little investigation the police discovered that Murray had in fact been involved in a botched robbery of a convenience store earlier that day. During the course of the robbery Murray had struggled with the clerk and the shotgun he was carrying went off, blasting away part of his hand. The one-armed bandit was arrested and taken to jail. You can count how many years in prison Murray got on one hand—in his case, you have to.

911 REPORT . . . 911 REPORT . . . 911 REPORT
REPORT . . . 911 REPORT . . . 911 RE
. . . 911 REPORT . . . 911 REPORT . . .
REPORT . . . 911 REPORT . . . 911 RE
ORT . . . 911 REPORT . . . 911 REPORT
REPORT . . . 911 REPORT . . . 911 RE
ORT . . . 911 REPORT . . . 911 REPORT
REPORT . . . 911 REPORT . . . 911 RE
ORT . . . 911 REPORT . . . 911 REPORT

"Where can
I get rid of my
Christmas tree?"

REPORT . . . 911 REPORT . . . 911 RE
ORT . . . 911 REPORT . . . 911 REPORT
REPORT . . . 911 REPORT . . . 911 RE
ORT . . . 911 REPORT . . . 911 REPORT
REPORT . . . 911 REPORT . . . 911 RE
ORT . . . 911 REPORT . . . 911 REPORT
REPORT . . . 911 REPORT . . . 911 RE
ORT . . . 911 REPORT . . . 911 REPORT

ORDERING TAKEOUT

DISPATCHER: Emergency line.

WOMAN: Hello, emergency police department? Um, I have someone out here that's going crazy. And they need to be taken away because they can't drive their self to the hospital.

DISPATCHER: They can't drive themself to the hospital?

WOMAN: That's right.

DISPATCHER: What kind of hospital, a mental hospital?

WOMAN: Yeah.

DISPATCHER: Can you drive him to the hospital?

WOMAN: No.

DISPATCHER: Is this a friend or relative?

WOMAN: No, it's me! And my parents won't take me, is what it is.

DISPATCHER: Well, call a taxi.

WOMAN: No, they have an emergency . . . this is an emer . . . they have an emergency take-away service.

DISPATCHER: Who?

WOMAN: Every city has an emergency take-away service, miss.

DISPATCHER: Not this city.

WOMAN: Fine. Thank you.

DISPATCHER: You're welcome.

FRICTION BURNS

The voice on the other end of the line was that of a small boy. He had called the emergency center in Charlotte, North Carolina, to report a fire. When the dispatcher asked for his name, the little boy hung up the phone. Glancing at the display screen, the dispatcher dialed the number where the emergency call had originated. A woman answered the phone and the officer asked her if there was a fire on her property. The woman was a little confused by the call but claimed there was no fire. The officer explained that the 911 center had received a call from a young boy at her address reporting a fire. The woman assured the police officer there was no fire but that as soon as she hung up, "There's going to be a fire on my son's backside."

"Can you unplug the coffeepot I left on at my house?"

JUST CALLING TO BRAG

DISPATCHER: Sheriff's office, can I help you?

MAN: Yes, can I have the officer in charge, please?

DISPATCHER: Okay, there aren't any deputies in here. What we'd have to do is take a name and a message or a number and have one of the sergeants call you . . . they're on the road. This is a communications building.

MAN: Okay. I just . . . I'm the guy who robs all your stores in Lakeland and I'm just letting you guys know that you ain't ever going to catch me, you stupid punks!

DISPATCHER: Okay.

LIKE FATHER, LIKE DAUGHTER

DISPATCHER: 911, what's the address of your emergency?

MALE CALLER: My daughter is suicidal, and she just left
              walking from Pebble Creek.

DISPATCHER: What does she look like?

MALE CALLER: She has brown hair, she's five months pregnant.

DISPATCHER: About how tall?

MALE CALLER: Oh, she's about my height.

TRYING TO GO OUT
WITH A BANG!

A 911 call alerted paramedics to a twenty-eight-year-old male who had attempted suicide. The man was brought into the emergency room where it was discovered he had swallowed several nitroglycerin pills (prescribed for a heart condition) as well as a quart of vodka. The man was questioned about the unusual bruises on his head and chest. He claimed the bruises were caused by his suicide attempt; he had slammed himself repeatedly into a wall in an effort to make the nitroglycerin pills explode.

-- 911 REPORT --

"I am watching my neighbor's dog.
It's in the garage. Should I let it in?"

WHEN YOU HEAR THE TONE, THE TIME WILL BE . . .

DISPATCHER: 911 emergency.

MAN: Yes, I'd like to know the day and date today.

DISPATCHER: I'm sorry, you what?

MAN: The day and date today.

DISPATCHER: Okay. Do you have an emergency?

MAN: Yes, I want to know the day and date today. That's all I know. I won't talk about it any further.

DISPATCHER: You just want to know what the day is?

MAN: Yeah.

DISPATCHER: Well, today's Saturday.

MAN: And it's the twenty-third?

DISPATCHER: Twenty-third.

MAN: Okay, thank you, ma'am.

DISPATCHER: Yeah, you're . . .

MAN: Bless you.

DISPATCHER: You're so welcome.

MAN: Good-bye.

DISPATCHER: Bye-bye.

AN EMERGENCY REQUEST

DISPATCHER: 911 emergency.

MAN: Oh, hello. Could I ask for a request?

DISPATCHER: Sure, what . . .

MAN: Play something by the Case Brothers, Martin and Gibson.

DISPATCHER: Who is this?

MAN: Is this [radio station call letters]?

DISPATCHER: This is the police department.

MAN: Oh, I got the wrong place.

NUTS OVER ANIMALS

esha Whyte walked out into her yard and discovered an injured squirrel lying near her home. She didn't know who to call—so she called 911. The dispatcher explained to Whyte three times that 911 was only for injured people and they didn't send out ambulances for animals. Whyte called again a little later and told the 911 operator that her house was on fire. "Officer Bill Smith ran out of his patrol car with his extinguisher, thinking there was a fire," Sergeant Dennis DePew said. "And she [Whyte] said there was never a fire, she just wanted someone to pick up that squirrel." Whyte was arrested and held in a minimum security prison for women. She was released the next day after posting six hundred dollars' bail. There is no record as to whether the squirrel posted her bail or not.

-- 911 REPORT --

"A neighbor's tree fell on my house.
The neighbors are not home. Will I get sued if I cut it up?"

WHERE'S THE TIDY BOWL MAN
WHEN YOU NEED HIM?

DISPATCHER: 911.

WOMAN: Uh, hi. This isn't an emergency, per se.
But I don't know who else to call.

DISPATCHER: Where are you?

WOMAN: We're on Highway 101 and there's a . . .

DISPATCHER: Going in which direction?

WOMAN: We're going south. But the thing I'm reporting
is that at the gas station and Mini-mart, the
public health officials really need to take a look
at that bathroom there.

DISPATCHER: Okay, you might want to call them, then.

WOMAN: I'm . . .

DISPATCHER: Was there an emergency? Does anyone need
an ambulance?

WOMAN: No, no. . . .

DISPATCHER: Does anyone need a fire truck?

WOMAN: No.

DISPATCHER: Okay, you just want to report a health hazard?

WOMAN: Yeah.

DISPATCHER: Okay, then you should call the health officials.

WOMAN: How would I—

DISPATCHER: If they're not in your phone book, call 411.

WOMAN: So I would have to pull off and find a phone booth, you guys can't report it?

DISPATCHER: Or call 411.

WOMAN: 411?

DISPATCHER: Yeah, you can call 411—Information.

WOMAN: You guys can't—

DISPATCHER: They'll have the phone numbers for you.

WOMAN: You can't report it?

DISPATCHER: This is a 911 line. For health problems you need to report it to the proper authorities.

WOMAN: Thank you.

DISPATCHER: Okay.

NOW THAT REALLY STINKS

What's black and white and foams at the mouth? That's right, a rabid skunk. According to an article in the *Salem* (Massachusetts) *Evening News*, fifty-one-year-old Carmen LaBrecque was in her backyard when a rabid skunk attacked her. She ran but the skunk ran after her—biting at her heels and cutting her off at every turn. This rabid round robin went on for nearly fifteen minutes. She couldn't slow down enough to open the back door and was forced to run around her house at least twelve times. During one of her trips her elderly mother leaned out of the door and handed her a cordless phone. LaBrecque used the phone to call 911, and soon an animal control officer was on the scene and subdued the smelling stalker. So it took a black and white to catch a black and white.

-- 911 REPORT --

"There's a baby cow running loose in my yard. You've got to kill it before it eats my children."

I SAID, HOLD THE ANCHOVIES!

DISPATCHER: 911, what's the address of your emergency?

MALE CALLER: I went out to dinner and brought home my leftover pizza, but I left it in the car, and this morning I went outside to get the pizza and it was soggy, but I didn't think anything of it. So I ate it and it tasted kind of funny, so I went back out to the car and noticed that the anti-freeze had spilled onto my pizza. Is that dangerous?

WITH A KNICK, KNACK,
PATTY-WHACK . . .

Sitting at her dinner table in the Los Angeles suburb of
Whittier, thirty-three-year-old Anna Mora didn't think twice
about giving her puppy a chicken bone—and the dog didn't
think twice about swallowing it. Soon the dog began to choke.
Not knowing what else to do or how to help her panicky pooch,
Mora called 911 to ask for help. Sheriff's Deputy James Stroud,
who answered the call, patiently talked Mora through instructions for the Heimlich maneuver. He told her to use an upward
thrusting motion under the dog's rib cage. That did the trick!
The bone popped out and the pup hopped down. "Owner and
puppy are both doing fine," said police spokesman Roger Horn.
"I guess this dog really had its day." I guess Mora is lucky she
didn't have to give the dog mouth-to-mouth resuscitation.

911 REPORT . . . 911 REPORT . . . 911 REPORT
. 911 REPORT . . . 911 REPORT . . . 911
RT . . . 911 REPORT . . . 911 REPORT
. 911 REPORT . . . 911 REPORT . . . 911
911 REPORT . . . 911 REPORT . . . 911 REP
. 911 REPORT . . . 911 REPORT . . . 911
911 REPORT . . . 911 REPORT . . . 911 REP

"Do I have to put money in the parking meters on Broadway?"

911 REPORT . . . 911 REPORT . . . 911 REP
. 911 REPORT . . . 911 REPORT . . . 911
911 REPORT . . . 911 REPORT . . . 911 REP
. 911 REPORT . . . 911 REPORT . . . 911
911 REPORT . . . 911 REPORT . . . 911 REP
. 911 REPORT . . . 911 REPORT . . . 911
911 REPORT . . . 911 REPORT . . . 911 REP

THE POSITIVE AND NEGATIVE
OF DISPATCHING

DISPATCHER: 911, can I help you?

OLDER FEMALE: Yes, can you tell me how to put batteries in my little fan here? It says I have a double-A battery and on it, it says "One Double-A Plus," and on the bottom it says "Plus Double-A One." How do I . . . how do I do that?

DISPATCHER: Well, did you open up the back where the batteries go in?

OLDER FEMALE: Pardon? I didn't hear you.

DISPATCHER: Did you open it up where the batteries go in?

OLDER FEMALE: Yes.

DISPATCHER: Okay, are there any directions as far as which one . . . do you see where the plus is?

OLDER FEMALE: I see where it's a little round, a little round wire.

DISPATCHER: Okay, hold on one second. Okay, are you having trouble putting them in the right way?

OLDER FEMALE: Yes I am. I don't know how to put them in.

DISPATCHER: Okay. Well, why don't you try putting them in . . . uh . . . make sure that the . . . You see the part where the bump is?

OLDER FEMALE: Right.

DISPATCHER: That should be where it says "plus."

OLDER FEMALE: Oh.

DISPATCHER: So wherever it says "plus," that should be where the bump is.

OLDER FEMALE: The top says "One Double-A Plus."

DISPATCHER: Okay, does it take one or two batteries?

OLDER FEMALE: Two.

DISPATCHER: Two batteries?

OLDER FEMALE: Yes. And the one at the bottom says "Plus Double-A One." And the battery has a plus on it and the other battery has a plus on it.

DISPATCHER: Well, the plus is referring to the side of the battery—like the top part, where the bump is.

OLDER FEMALE: I see. Put them in the same way?

DISPATCHER: Put them in exactly the same way. If that doesn't work take them out and switch them around and see if that works.

OLDER FEMALE: Okay.

DISPATCHER: All right.

OLDER FEMALE: Thank you, ma'am.

DISPATCHER: You're so welcome.

OLDER FEMALE: God bless you.

DISPATCHER: God bless you, too.

OLDER FEMALE: Okay, bye-bye.

DISPATCHER: Bye-bye.

PLEASE DON'T LITTER
IN MY HOUSE

DISPATCHER: 911, fire or emergency.

MAN: Hard to tell. Not really an emergency, I guess.

DISPATCHER: What's the problem there, sir?

MAN: Well, a cat just walked into the house I am in and gave birth to kittens!

DISPATCHER: Sir?

MAN: Kittens, you know. What do I do? Should I wash them? They look like they need to be washed.

DISPATCHER: I'll connect you to animal control.

MAN: But should I wash them?

GUEST BATHROOM

perators at 911 centers have received complaints about clogged toilets before, but the call the Mesa, Arizona, 911 dispatchers received from Jona Giammalva rattled even them. Giammalva was angry at her children because she thought they had flushed one of their toys down the toilet. Try as she might, Giammalva couldn't get the toilet to flush properly. She tried drain clearer, a wire coat hanger, and a plunger. Finally, after several tries, Giammalva saw something slowly emerging from the toilet. Was it a piece of Lego? A small truck, perhaps? She leaned in closer to get a better look and was soon face to face with a huge boa constrictor. "I was out of there in a split second," Giammalva said. "I wasn't about to waste any time."

She quickly called 911 and was referred to a wildlife expert. The expert arrived and soon had the toilet bowl boa out of the bathroom and out of Giammalva's house. Both the snake and Giammalva let out a sigh of relief. How cruel to have a snake in your toilet right after you've gotten the crap scared out of you.

-- 911 REPORT --

"Yeah, my neighbors are making way too much noise praying."

ESPRIT DE CORPSE

DISPATCHER: Operator.

MAN: Yes, I've got a dead body over here in front of my house.

DISPATCHER: How do you know it's dead?

MAN: 'Cause the boy across the street in the lot is hollering for somebody to call the police.
He's yelling, "Call the police! Call the police!"

DISPATCHER: He is dead? Is he shot?

MAN: He said he's dead, miss. 113 North Munt.

DISPATCHER: Well, we get a lot of dead bodies, sometimes . . .

MAN: Well, you hear the guy calling "help" now?

OTHER VOICE: *Help!*

DISPATCHER: All right, we'll be there. Thanks.

MAN: Damn.

FIRST TIME FOR EVERYTHING

DISPATCHER: 911.

CALLER: Help! Help! Send the police! I been shot!

DISPATCHER: You said you've been shot?

CALLER: I been shot!

DISPATCHER: How many times were you shot?

CALLER: This be the first time!

911 REPORT ... 911 REPORT ... 911 REPORT
911 REPORT ... 911 REPORT ... 911 RE
... 911 REPORT ... 911 REPORT ...
911 REPORT ... 911 REPORT ... 911 RE
PORT ... 911 REPORT ... 911 REPORT
911 REPORT ... 911 REPORT ... 911 RE

"My upstairs
neighbor's bed
is squeaking too
damn loud!"

911 REPORT ... 911 REPORT ... 911 RE
PORT ... 911 REPORT ... 911 REPORT
911 REPORT ... 911 REPORT ... 911 RE
PORT ... 911 REPORT ... 911 REPORT
911 REPORT ... 911 REPORT ... 911 RE
PORT ... 911 REPORT ... 911 REPORT

PHONE SEX

Portage, Indiana, police dispatchers received a 911 call in which the caller never spoke, but shrieks and screams could be heard in the background. A squad car was dispatched to the residence with a "possible assault in progress" call. The officers quickly arrived on the scene and discovered the reason for all the screaming. The couple living at the house had accidentally knocked off the receiver while they were having sex. Maybe they took the phone company slogan "Reach out and touch someone" seriously.

YOU THINK IT'S FUNNY,
BUT IT'S SNOT

DISPATCHER: 911, what's the address of your emergency?

CITIZEN: I need to know what I can do about someone who came into my home and put boogers on my wall.

DISPATCHER: Did you invite this person into your home?

CITIZEN: Yes, but I didn't give him permission to put boogers on the walls.

YOU'RE OUR FOURTH CALLER . . .

DISPATCHER: 911, fire or emergency?

WOMAN: I need the number to [local radio station].

DISPATCHER: Ma'am, 911 is for emergency purposes only.

WOMAN: I know that, I need it right away!

DISPATCHER: That doesn't qualify as an emergency situation, ma'am.

WOMAN: Dammit! I know the *&%# answer to their trivia question but I don't remember their *&^# number!

TALKING OUT OF
BOTH SIDES OF HIS FACE

Michelle Chasse, a Panama City Police Department dispatcher, picked up the phone when a 911 call came in, but there was no one on the other line. The screen displayed the address where the call was made and the phone was listed under a woman's name. Protocol demands 911 operators call back any hang-ups, and that's exactly what Chasse did. But when Chasse dialed the number, a man answered the phone.

"He said it was a mistake, and I said, 'Let me speak to [the woman],' and he said, 'Just a minute' then he left and came back and was disguising his voice as a female," she said. "It was kind of creepy.

"And he said, 'Hi, this is Shirley,' and, of course, I know this is him," she continued. She also told him she recognized his voice. "He said, 'Okay, just a minute.' And he left and came back and still tried to act like she was there—and by this time we had officers on the way—'This is she. What's the problem? Everything's fine.'"

When police arrived they discovered the owner of the house was being held against her will by the double-talking man. Soon a fight broke out when police attempted to take the man into custody. I guess he couldn't talk his way out of that one.

-- 911 REPORT --

"Is it okay for a man to go to work in women's clothing?"

ON THE RIGHT TRACK

[The sounds of screaming and a loud rumbling sound]

DISPATCHER: 911 emergency. 911 emergency. Hello?

[The dispatcher calls back.]

WOMAN: Hello?

DISPATCHER: This is 911, do you have an emergency there?

WOMAN: No, I'm sorry, I don't. I must have hit the wrong button. I'm sorry.

DISPATCHER: Okay, ma'am, do you have your 911 button on a speed dial?

WOMAN: I didn't think I did. But I'll certainly look at it and turn it off if it is.

DISPATCHER: Were you on a roller coaster or what?

WOMAN: Yeah, I was on a ride.

DISPATCHER: Because I heard a lot of excited "whooos."

WOMAN: Yeah.

DISPATCHER: Yeah.

WOMAN: Okay.

DISPATCHER: Okay, bye-bye.

HOPPING MAD

DISPATCHER: 911. What is your emergency?

FEMALE CALLER: I am trapped in my house.

DISPATCHER: Trapped? Is someone holding you there?

FEMALE CALLER: Someone? No. But there is a frog on the front porch.

DISPATCHER: A frog?

FEMALE CALLER: Yes, a frog.

DISPATCHER: Okay, but what is preventing you from leaving the house?

FEMALE CALLER: I told you. There is a frog on the porch and I am afraid of frogs.

DISPATCHER: And you don't have another door to the house?

FEMALE CALLER: No. There is only one door and I can't get out of the house with the frog sitting there.

DISPATCHER: Why don't you take a broom and sweep the frog off the porch?

FEMALE CALLER: I can't do that. I told you, I am afraid of frogs. He might get me.

DISPATCHER: Um . . . I'm not sure how I can help you with this.

FEMALE CALLER: Can't you send a police officer over here to move the frog?

DISPATCHER: No, ma'am. I can't send a police officer or a warden out for this.

UP ON THE HOUSETOP, CLICK, CLICK, CLICK

Little Cindy Lou Who finding the Grinch in her house was nothing compared to the Christmas visitor spotted by a neighbor in Vancouver. Santa Claus, complete with beard and red suit, was toting a shotgun instead of a bag of goodies and was seen sneaking into a house with two accomplices. The neighbor quickly called 911 to report that this appearance of Santa "a few days before Christmas gave him "clause" for concern. Police car sirens apparently frightened away the jolly fat man and his two elves—but not before they had tied up the occupants of the house and ransacked the place. Police soon discovered why Santa had made his little visit—the house had an elaborate marijuana-growing operation in the basement. I always wondered what Santa had in that little corncob pipe. Maybe that's why he's so jolly.

-- 911 REPORT --

"I parked my car in a spot that says
TRUCK LOADING & UNLOADING ONLY, TOWAWAY ZONE.
What is going to happen to my car?"

SORRY, I'M ALL
TIED UP AT THE MOMENT

DISPATCHER:	911.
MAN:	[very garbled] I am a victim of a robbery. I'm in my house and I'm gagged and tied up with extension cord and I need the police.
DISPATCHER:	Sir, I can't understand you.
OTHER DISPATCHER:	He said he's the victim of a robbery, he's been tied up and gagged.
DISPATCHER:	Where's he at?
OTHER DISPATCHER:	Can you give us your address?
MAN:	600 [unintelligible].
DISPATCHER:	600 what?
MAN:	[unintelligible]
DISPATCHER:	Walnut? Orange?
MAN:	No, [unintelligible].
DISPATCHER:	Olive . . . Olive . . . Olive, sir?

MAN: [unintelligible]

OTHER DISPATCHER: Olive? Uh, you want me to have the operator, you want me to have someone check this out?

DISPATCHER: Please.

MAN: [unintelligible] in a hurry . . .

DISPATCHER: I understand, sir. 600 Olive. Are you saying "Olive"?

MAN: [unintelligible]

DISPATCHER: I can't figure out what he's saying. Is it Atlantic?

MAN: [unintelligible] . . . like the nut. A-l-m-o-n-d.

DISPATCHER: Almond! Almond, right? 600 Almond. Okay, it won't be necessary. You won't have to run a check. How long ago did this happen?

MAN: [unintelligible]

DISPATCHER: Okay, listen to me, listen to me. Do you live in a house or an apartment there?

MAN: An apartment.

DISPATCHER: What apartment do you live in?

MAN: One, two.

DISPATCHER: One, two. All right, which . . .

MAN: [unintelligible] Two!

DISPATCHER: What apartment?

MAN: *Two!*

DISPATCHER: Two? Okay. And what's his last name?

MAN: [unintelligible]

DISPATCHER: Okay, sir, we're going to send the police out, all right?

MAN: [unintelligible] quick [unintelligible] tied up with extension cord . . .

DISPATCHER: All right . . . bye-bye . . . sir, let me go so I can send the police, all right?

MAN: [unintelligible]

DISPATCHER: Bye-bye.

A CUT ABOVE THE REST

In August 1995, nineteen-year-old Jerry Wilson called 911 to report someone had broken into an apartment. It wasn't his apartment, and he wasn't the neighbor, either—he was the burglar. When Wilson broke into the Charleston, West Virginia, apartment window to gain access, he cut himself so badly he was in desperate need of medical attention. Paramedics arrived and helped Wilson to the hospital—later, the police helped Wilson to jail.

-- 911 REPORT --

"The doctor told me I had a twenty-four-hour virus.
How long will it last?"

AN ALARMING ALARM SYSTEM

It's a system that Rube Goldberg would be proud of. Apparently, there is no central system of flashing alarms, bells, or warnings in Detroit's firehouses, according to the *Detroit News*, which was leading an investigation. How are the firefighters warned when an alarm is called in? Simple. Well, not so simple—but here's how it works. Each station is equipped with a dot-matrix printer, and firefighters have placed a lead weight on the paper feed, which is tied to a switch that activates a warning bell. The printer automatically engages when a 911 dispatcher sends a message to the firehouse computers. When the paper moves it pushes off the weight, which falls. When the string to which it is attached goes taut, it pulls the switch, which rings the bell. Was this system set up temporarily while an electronic or more modern alarm system is installed? Nope; it's been that way for fifteen years. And according to Detroit Fire Commissioner Charles Wilson, there are no plans to replace the system, because it's always worked pretty well. And like they say . . . (See title of next story.)

IF IT AIN'T BROKE—DON'T FIX IT

DISPATCHER: 911, what's your emergency?

WOMAN: Well, I just need some advice [giggle].

DISPATCHER: What can I help you with, ma'am?

WOMAN: It's a little embarrassing, but you're a woman, right?

DISPATCHER: Yes, ma'am. Do you have an emergency?

WOMAN: Well . . . I just had a baby and the doctor told me to do those Kegel exercises—you know, to tighten up things down there [giggle].

DISPATCHER: Yes, ma'am, I understand. Are you in pain?

WOMAN: No, no, no. It's not that. It's just that every time I do those exercises I have an orgasm.

DISPATCHER: I'm sorry, did you say "orgasm"?

WOMAN: Yes. Am I doing them right?

DISPATCHER: Sounds like it to me.

BEING COTTONTAILED

Here comes Peter Cottontail, hopping down the crime trail. Barry Gibson, a dental technician, was dressed out in full bunny outfit—long ears, fluffy tail, and whiskers—to promote his wife's shop in Ellicott City, Maryland. Mr. Gibson's rabbit ears served as an antenna to crime when two thieves walked into his wife's store, the Forget-Me-Not Factory. He noticed the woman slip a wooden Christmas ornament into her purse and then quickly exit the store. Carrots must have served his eyesight well, because Gibson followed the couple as they entered five more shops—each time relieving the store of a piece of merchandise. Apparently, the two shoplifters never ate carrots—they didn't notice a huge rabbit following them from store to store. At the last shop Gibson alerted the manager, who dialed 911. *That* must have been a call: "Uh, excuse me. But a large rabbit has just told me that there has been a string of shoplifting done by two people and they're in my store now." "Sure. You're not talking about your pal Harvey, are you?" However the phone call went, police arrived and arrested the shoplifting team and took them to the Howard County Detention Center. After they realized they had been tailed by a bunny, how mad do you think they were? Hopping, perhaps?

ATLAS SHRUGGED

DISPATCHER: 911, fire or emergency?

WOMAN: I want to file a complaint.

DISPATCHER: What's the problem?

WOMAN: There's these two a**holes who've been following me around.

DISPATCHER: I'm sorry?

WOMAN: What's your (&^% problem, lady? There's two guys who were following me in their car and I want them arrested.

DISPATCHER: Did they hurt you?

WOMAN: No, they didn't do nothing. There's just pests and I want you to bust their asses.

DISPATCHER: Where are they now?

WOMAN:	How the hell should I know?
DISPATCHER:	Where are you?
WOMAN:	In my living room.
DISPATCHER:	Where?
WOMAN:	In my living room, in my house.
DISPATCHER:	What is your address?
WOMAN:	316.
DISPATCHER:	316 what?
WOMAN:	316 North, a**hole!
DISPATCHER:	I'm sorry, that's not a valid street in this city.

THE WOMAN WITH THE GREEN THUMB

Staten Island, New York, native Yolanda Watson panicked when she discovered she couldn't get out of her own bedroom. The lock had jammed and the door was stuck shut. She banged on the door, but try as she might, she couldn't get out. Thankfully, she had a phone in the bedroom and she quickly called 911 for assistance. In a matter of minutes the police arrived and helped the stranded woman out of her bedroom. On their way out, after a job well done, the police glanced around Watson's apartment. It was your typical New York apartment except for one thing—or should I say 195 things. Police confiscated 195 marijuana plants that Watson was growing in her living room. The next time Watson was behind a door that was locked, it was inside a jail cell.

-- 911 REPORT --

"I lost a hundred dollars tonight
playing poker, and now I'm nervous."

DO YOU KISS YOUR MOTHER WITH THAT MOUTH?

DISPATCHER: Emergency.

WOMAN: Son of a ****, don't you ever hang up on me again!

DISPATCHER: Ma'am, what's the problem?

WOMAN: You just hung up on me.

DISPATCHER: No, I didn't talk to you. What's the problem?

WOMAN: The one I was talking to, she hung up on me. And I don't go for that *$@!

DISPATCHER: Ma'am, she was answering 911 life-and-death emergency calls. What's your emergency?

WOMAN: I bet, I bet. You tell her not to ever hang up on me again. I'm a citizen of the United States. I have a right to complain. And if you just don't like it, you're going to get a complaint . . .

DISPATCHER: All right, make sure you follow that up with the traffic division, okay?

THE OTHER WHITE MEAT

An obviously hungry and irate Darryl Evans called the 911 operator in Slidell, Louisiana, and requested police assistance in getting his mother to cook him a pork-chop dinner. When the dispatcher explained to Evans he was tying up an emergency line on a frivolous call, the man became more and more upset. He argued back and forth with the operator, claiming his call was an emergency and that he really needed the pork chops. Evans became increasingly vulgar and abusive with the operator until she finally dispatched a unit to investigate the call. Evans was arrested and charged with disorderly conduct. I wonder how he felt once he realized what was on the prison menu that night: meatloaf.

REPORT . . . 911 REPORT . . . 911 REP
. 911 REPORT . . . 911 REPORT . . . 911
RT . . . 911 REPORT . . . 911 REPORT
. 911 REPORT . . . 911 REPORT . . . 91
REPORT . . . 911 REPORT . . . 911 REP
. 911 REPORT . . . 911 REPORT . . . 911

**"Somebody's left
an unattended car
out on the street
for two weeks."**

. 911 REPORT . . . 911 REPORT . . . 911
REPORT . . . 911 REPORT . . . 911 REP
. 911 REPORT . . . 911 REPORT . . . 911
REPORT . . . 911 REPORT . . . 911 REP
. 911 REPORT . . . 911 REPORT . . . 911
REPORT . . . 911 REPORT . . . 911 REP

DOWN IN THE MOUTH

DISPATCHER: 911 emergency.

MAN: I don't know what . . . some—something is happening, uh, to me right now, I don't know what is going on. It's just . . . I, I . . . it's hard to explain. Just things are just growing out of my mouth. And I am not calling . . . this is no joke.

DISPATCHER: Did you need the police or do you need an ambulance?

MAN: I need the ambulance. I need to go to the hospital because something . . . things are just growing in my mouth.

DISPATCHER: Like what?

MAN: I don't know what . . .

DISPATCHER: Okay, hold on. Let me connect you to an ambulance.

[Phone rings and is picked up.]

FIRE DEPARTMENT: Fire department.

MAN: Uh, yes. I don't know what is going on, but something is growing . . . things are growing in my mouth.

[long pause]

FIRE DEPARTMENT:	Things are growing in your mouth?
MAN:	Yes, I don't know what is going on. I was in the bed and now things are growing in my mouth.
FIRE DEPARTMENT:	Things are growing in your mouth?
MAN:	Yes.
FIRE DEPARTMENT:	What kind of things are growing in your mouth?
MAN:	I don't know what they are. I can't see them.
FIRE DEPARTMENT:	Can you feel them [cough], feel them?
MAN:	Well, yes, I feel them in my mouth, but I don't know what they are.
FIRE DEPARTMENT:	What do they feel like? Do they feel like trees? Or . . .
MAN:	Or just . . .
FIRE DEPARTMENT:	. . . limbs, or what?
MAN:	Like circles.
FIRE DEPARTMENT:	Like circles . . .
MAN:	Like little balls or something, I don't know what they are.
FIRE DEPARTMENT:	Have you looked in the mirror?
MAN:	I'm afraid to!

JUST ONE MORE TIME
FOR GOOD MEASURE

Javier R. Curbeira was seen happily loading a truck with the burglarized belongings of a home on New World Drive in San Antonio, Texas. Neighbors were a little suspicious about seeing a stranger loading up a truck with their neighbor's things and they quickly called 911. Curbeira was arrested and then later released on bond the next afternoon. According to the police, only a short four hours after his release, Curbeira was back in the same driveway, this time with a different truck, loading up the same burglarized stuff. You guessed it—the same neighbors called 911 and Curbeira was rearrested. I've heard of a repeat offender—but not one who repeats exactly the same offense.

-- 911 REPORT --

"I think my teenage daughter is having sex,
and I want her to be checked."

QUIET DOWN, CLASS

DISPATCHER: 911.

MAN: Yeah, you have got people working in the school right now. And they've been working all night long violating the noise code over here.

DISPATCHER: Sir, if you're reporting a noise complaint that's not an emergency call. You'll have to call on the business line.

MAN: Really?

DISPATCHER: Yes, really. This is for emergency calls only.

MAN: Well, how about if I shoot them, would it be an emergency then?

DISPATCHER: Sure would.

MAN: All right.

DISPATCHER: But you'll have to call back on the business line. Thank you.

NO ROOM TO SPARE

In April 1997, Janet Stewart was driving down a road in Victoria, Texas, when suddenly her car got a flat tire. She pulled over to the side of the road hoping a motorist would stop to help her; no one showed up. Not knowing how to change a tire herself, she used her cell phone to call 911. Soon a team of police officers arrived and told Stewart they would gladly help her change the tire. The officers asked if it was okay to open her trunk to get out the jack and spare tire. Stewart said it was fine, and when the cops popped the trunk they discovered something that wasn't standard equipment— 118 pounds of marijuana. Police asked why she had allowed them to open her trunk when she knew it was filled with pot? Stewart admitted she thought the officers would bring their own jack and therefore wouldn't have to open her trunk. Seems like Stewart is one jack shy of a full deck.

REPORT . . . 911 REPORT . . . 911 REP
. 911 REPORT . . . 911 REPORT . . . 911
RT . . . 911 REPORT . . . 911 REPORT
. 911 REPORT . . . 911 REPORT . . . 911
REPORT . . . 911 REPORT . . . 911 REP
. 911 REPORT . . . 911 REPORT . . . 911
REPORT . . . 911 REPORT . . . 911 REP

"I took a laxative
last night, and now
I have diarrhea."

REPORT . . . 911 REPORT . . . 911 REP
. 911 REPORT . . . 911 REPORT . . . 911
REPORT . . . 911 REPORT . . . 911 REP
. 911 REPORT . . . 911 REPORT . . . 911
REPORT . . . 911 REPORT . . . 911 REP
. 911 REPORT . . . 911 REPORT . . . 911
REPORT . . . 911 REPORT . . . 911 REP

HE'S A REAL LEG MAN

DISPATCHER: 911 emergency.

MAN: Uh, look, uh, I live in a mobile home.

DISPATCHER: Uh-huh.

MAN: I live in a mobile home park.

DISPATCHER: Okay, are you needing the police, fire, or paramedics, sir?

MAN: Huh? I don't know what I need.

DISPATCHER: Okay, you called 911. Do you need an ambulance?

MAN: My legs, they itch so bad, I think I'm going to go crazy.

DISPATCHER: Okay. Your legs itch very bad?

MAN: Are you listening to me?

DISPATCHER: I sure am.

MAN: All right now. My legs are itching so bad that they are driving me crazy.

DISPATCHER: Okay, would you like to speak to the paramedics?

MAN: Yes, I would like to speak to them please.

[Dispatcher transfers call to the fire department.]

FIRE DEPARTMENT: Fire emergency.

MAN: Hello, is this the medics?

FIRE DEPARTMENT: This is the fire department.

MAN: The fire department?

FIRE DEPARTMENT: Uh-huh, what did you need?

MAN: I have no fire. I have no fire.

FIRE DEPARTMENT: Okay, do you need paramedics?

MAN: Excuse me?

FIRE DEPARTMENT: Do you need paramedics?

MAN: I don't know whether I need paramedics.
                  I don't know.

FIRE DEPARTMENT: What's the problem?

MAN: My legs. My legs are itching something
                  terrible. It's been this way for two or three
                  days now.

FIRE DEPARTMENT: Okay . . .

MAN: Now look. It's not an emergency.

FIRE DEPARTMENT:	It's okay, we can come out and check you out. Can you tell me how old you are?
MAN:	Excuse me, please?
FIRE DEPARTMENT:	Can you tell me how old you are?
MAN:	Am I what?
FIRE DEPARTMENT:	How old are you?
MAN:	How old am I?
FIRE DEPARTMENT:	Yes.
MAN:	I'm eighty-three. I'll be eighty-three years old pretty soon.
FIRE DEPARTMENT:	Okay, how is your breathing?
MAN:	My breathing is fine. Geez, my legs itch me something terrible.
FIRE DEPARTMENT:	Is there a rash on it?
MAN:	A rash? That's right. I've been to the doctor and I've got a rash on my legs—do you understand?
FIRE DEPARTMENT:	Uh-huh.
MAN:	I'm not going crazy. I have all my marbles. You understand?
FIRE DEPARTMENT:	Are you nauseous or have you been vomiting?
MAN:	Excuse me, please?

FIRE DEPARTMENT: Are you nauseous or have you been vomiting?

MAN: No. No vomiting, nothing like that. My legs itch. I just want . . . my legs itch.

FIRE DEPARTMENT: Okay, I just need you to answer a couple of questions. Are you pale, cool, or sweaty?

MAN: Am I what?

FIRE DEPARTMENT: Are you pale, cool, or sweaty?

MAN: No, no, nothing like that. It's just that my legs itch.

FIRE DEPARTMENT: Is there any pain with that?

MAN: Any pain?

FIRE DEPARTMENT: Uh-huh.

MAN: Just a dull, bad itch.

FIRE DEPARTMENT: Okay, we'll be right there, okay?

MAN: All right, now, look, I don't want to spend a lot of money on nylons and things like that. Because it isn't so. My legs itch me very bad.

FIRE DEPARTMENT: You can tell the paramedics that when they get there. Okay?

MAN: Okay, thank you.

FIRE DEPARTMENT: Okay, bye-bye.

A HIGHER CALLING

When a morning shift employee of the Valley Cafe in Denver, Colorado, opened up the restaurant at five A.M. he heard the panicked shout of "Help me, help me." The employee called 911. When police arrived they looked around but didn't immediately locate the source of the screaming—until they looked up. What they saw was six-foot-two, 175-pound Lawrence VanCleave, wearing nothing but his socks, stuck in the kitchen vent. According to Detective Ralph Bravo, the twenty-six-year-old man was wedged in the fourteen-inch-diameter pipe. Since he was so tall, VanCleave's arms were sticking out of the vent's opening on the roof, next to his clothes. His torso was stuck in the middle of the vent and his stocking feet were dangling from the opening in the ceiling. (Other things were dangling too, but I won't go into that.) Apparently, VanCleave had been stuck that way for about five hours. Rescue workers had to spray WD-40 into the vent in order to help the naked VanCleave slip out. He was arrested for attempted burglary. My question is, if the man was stuck in a restaurant, why did rescuers have to use WD-40 when there was a grease pit right there?

-- 911 REPORT --

"My husband won't let me turn the heat on in the house."

BABY POTLUCK

DISPATCHER: 911.

YOUNG FEMALE: Yeah, hi.

DISPATCHER: Do you have an emergency, ma'am?

YOUNG FEMALE: I hope not. It's just . . .

DISPATCHER: What are you reporting?

YOUNG FEMALE: Well, I'll just lay it out for you, okay?

DISPATCHER: Uh-huh.

YOUNG FEMALE: You see, my husband and I—I don't have to give you his name, right?

DISPATCHER: It depends . . .

YOUNG FEMALE: Anyway, we've been trying to get pregnant, you know, for like, four months now.

DISPATCHER: Ma'am, are you calling to report an emergency?

YOUNG FEMALE: It's just, you see, I've been smoking a lot of pot lately and I'm wondering if that might be, you know, why things haven't happened.

DISPATCHER: What things?

YOUNG FEMALE: You know, the fetus thing.

LET YOUR FINGERS
DO THE WALKING

Twenty-four-year-old Hugo Murdock, a migrant fruit picker from Quebec, was helping himself to a tank full of someone else's gas courtesy of a siphon hose. After he had drained the tank he realized the hose had gotten stuck in the tank, so he stuck his little finger inside the tank opening to free the hose. Bad move. Both the hose and Murdock's little finger were trapped when a spring-loaded flap inside the gas tank clamped down on them. Murdock couldn't get his finger out. His accomplices couldn't get his finger out. So they did the next best thing—they ran away. Not wanting their friend to stay stuck red-handed—or red-fingered—they decided the noble thing would be to call 911 and report Murdock's problem. An ambulance was the first on the scene, but the paramedics couldn't get Murdock's finger out of the tank. Police arrived soon after, but they couldn't get Murdock's finger out either. Firefighters moved the van, with Murdock still stuck, onto the street, to give them more room to cut off a portion of the gas tank pipe. Murdock was still stuck to the pipe, but at least now the pipe wasn't attached to the rest of the van.

Murdock and his pipe were taken to a local hospital, where doctors were finally able to free him. Although his pinkie was free, Murdock wasn't—he was taken to jail. He was sentenced to time served, eight months probation, and twenty hours of community service. He was also ordered to pay five hundred dollars to get the van repaired. When Murdock was sentenced I wonder if he thought about giving the judge the finger—or maybe even fingering his accomplices.

-- 911 REPORT --

"Yeah, I called earlier asking why my power was out,
and you said it was because of the storm.
If that's so, how come I saw a car drive by my house
a few minutes ago, and its lights were on?"

IN THIRTY MINUTES OR LESS

DISPATCHER: 911, what's the address of your emergency?

CITIZEN: My new wife left me and took all my clothes.

DISPATCHER: Okay, we can send an officer to take a theft report.

CITIZEN: Could you have the officer stop and get a pizza on his way over?

WAKE UP AND
SMELL THE COFFEE

DISPATCHER: 911. What is your emergency?

FEMALE CALLER: Is this the police?

DISPATCHER: Yes. Do you have an emergency?

FEMALE CALLER: Are you working the night shift?

DISPATCHER: I am tonight. Do you have an emergency I can help you with?

FEMALE CALLER: No. But would you give me a wake-up call at six A.M.?

DISPATCHER: Excuse me?

FEMALE CALLER: I need a wake-up call at six in the morning. I have an important doctor's appointment tomorrow and would like a wake-up call so I don't miss it.

DISPATCHER: Um, no, ma'am. I can't do that. Sorry.

A STEELY-EYED DOG

It was a cold and snowy evening when a frantic elderly woman called the communications center in Minot, North Dakota. The call was quickly answered and the woman on the other end started crying. She choked back tears and explained to the dispatcher that she was heartbroken because her neighbor's dog had frozen to death. "They moved away and left that poor, sweet puppy out in the cold. And now it's dead. How can people be so mean?"

The dispatcher tried calming the woman, but the woman insisted a police unit be dispatched to pick up the frozen dog and dispose of it properly. "I just fed him yesterday! He's in the front yard and hasn't moved all day. He's frozen standing straight up!"

The dispatcher, who was also an animal lover, sent one of the newer deputies to do a "welfare check" on a possible 10-7: (dead) dog.

As it was such a bone-chilling night, the deputy was reluctant to leave his warm squad car and trudge through the ice and snow to check on a dead dog—but he did. He arrived at the older woman's house, took her statement, and then went next door to check on the dog. Soon he radioed back to the communications center with his report. "The dog is 10-4, dispatch. Advise the woman that a cast-iron weenie dog doesn't require much shelter."

I wonder if the woman considered calling the police about the sad, frozen dwarf the neighbors left in their garden?

-- 911 REPORT --

"Can you look in the reverse phone book and give me the phone numbers for all of my mom's neighbors?"

DON'T DO WHAT I DO—
DO WHAT I SAY!

DISPATCHER: 911 emergency.

YOUNG BOY: Uh, my brother locked my mom out.

DISPATCHER: Your brother locked your mom out?

YOUNG BOY: Yeah.

DISPATCHER: Anybody else in the house with you?

YOUNG BOY: Only my brother.

DISPATCHER: I'm sorry . . .

YOUNG BOY: Bye!

DISPATCHER: Wait! Wait!

YOUNG BOY: What?

DISPATCHER: Your mom's outside and you're in the house
by yourself?

YOUNG BOY: No. [Hangs up]

[Dispatcher calls back number.]

WOMAN: Hello?

DISPATCHER: Hi, this is the police department. Someone just called 911. Your son?

WOMAN: My son?

DISPATCHER: Yeah.

WOMAN: A little boy?

DISPATCHER: Yeah, he said his mom was locked outside.

WOMAN: I can't believe he did that. I'm washing clothes in the back. And he said, "I'm going to lock you out." I said, "If you do, I'm going to call the police."

DISPATCHER: Oh, so he called.

WOMAN: Yeah.

DISPATCHER: So everything's okay there?

WOMAN: Yeah, sorry.

REACH OUT AND
TOUCH YOURSELF

Dispatchers at 911 centers across the United States get unique requests every day. Most of the time they can answer the person's question or at least direct him to someone who can. But when Ron Vanname called 911 nine times in sixteen minutes, what he requested couldn't be fulfilled by the operators (at least over the phone). In fact, in can't even be printed here. Vanname was arrested for making obscene phone calls to dispatchers from a phone booth in Port Charles, Florida. Guys like this aren't only perverts, they're also cheap. 911 can be dialed from a pay phone for no charge.

TECHNICAL FOUL

This call took place on Super Bowl Sunday, 2001.

DISPATCHER: 911. What is your emergency?

MALE CALLER: Is this the police department?

DISPATCHER: Yes. Do you have an emergency?

MALE CALLER: No. Is your TV on?

DISPATCHER: Yes . . .

MALE CALLER: What was the final score of the game?

JUST THE FAX, MA'AM

DISPATCHER: 911.

MAN: I need to speak to Chris a minute, please.

DISPATCHER: I'm sorry, who do you need?

MAN: Chris!

DISPATCHER: This is 911, did you need the police?

MAN: Uh, yes, ma'am, I sure do.

DISPATCHER: Well, who's Chris?

MAN: He was the policeman that did all my paperwork.

DISPATCHER: Uh-huh.

MAN: I think I need the assistance of emergency. I'm dialing 9 plus 911. I've got an immediate fax to get to the doctor immediately. And the hotel is not cooperating with me. It's for two whole bucks' worth of money. There's two dollars cash in this room somewhere but I can't find it. I've got to get a fax off to the doctor. Now, I'm told by your police department that when I needed them at the right time they'd come and take care of the situation. Is that true or is that a lie?

DISPATCHER: Let me just verify why you're calling. You're calling 911 . . .

MAN: Yes ma'am, 9 plus 911 . . .

DISPATCHER: Yeah, okay . . .

MAN: Got an emergency . . .

DISPATCHER: You have an emergency because you need to send a fax . . .

MAN: For two bucks.

DISPATCHER: Do you need the paramedics or something?

MAN: That would be good.

DISPATCHER: Okay. So you need the paramedics to respond to the hotel?

MAN: Provided they got two bucks to lend me until I can get to the bank and get my 923 . . .

DISPATCHER: Uh, you know what, that's not going to happen.

MAN: What's going to happen? Where am I going to get the damn two dollars from? Doesn't Dr. —'s name have any clout, even in this town? Isn't he — Grove's most prominent citizen? Am I going to go to work for him full time? Isn't that why I came here to begin with? I think so.

DISPATCHER: Okay, well, I don't have two bucks to lend, sir, so I'm not sure what to tell you.

MAN: Tell me where I can find two measly dollars in this town.

DISPATCHER: I don't know, sir.

MAN: I'll find it!

DISPATCHER: Uh-huh.

MAN: Bye.

DISPATCHER: Good-night.

... 911 REPORT ... 911 REPORT
1 REPORT ... 911 REPORT ... 911 RE
... 911 REPORT ... 911 REPORT ...
1 REPORT ... 911 REPORT ... 911 RE
PORT ... 911 REPORT ... 911 REPORT
1 REPORT ... 911 REPORT ... 911 RE
PORT ... 911 REPORT ... 911 REPORT

"Yes, I have a woman
here who is harassing
my front door."

PORT ... 911 REPORT ... 911 REPORT
1 REPORT ... 911 REPORT ... 911 RE
PORT ... 911 REPORT ... 911 REPORT
1 REPORT ... 911 REPORT ... 911 RE
PORT ... 911 REPORT ... 911 REPORT
1 REPORT ... 911 REPORT ... 911 RE
PORT ... 911 REPORT ... 911 REPORT

CANINE-ONE-ONE

Judi Bayly was sleeping soundly on a quiet night in March 1996 when her oxygen mask slipped off. Bayly, who has a breathing disorder, had lapsed into an asthma attack but didn't wake up. An alarm went off, and that's when her eight-year-old Irish setter, Lyric, leaped into action. The dog first tried to wake the sleeping Bayly with snout and tongue—but she wouldn't rouse. Lyric ran to the kitchen, knocked the phone off the hook, and bumped a speed-dial button on the phone three times to dial 911. "It's amazing," said Charlene Hall, a dispatcher at Nashua Fire Rescue in New Hampshire. "The dog is trained to go over and hit that phone three times to get 911 and she barks into the receiver." According to the emergency team, Bayly would have died if Lyric, a specially trained medical assistance dog, hadn't called 911. "I've got some kind of guardian angel sleeping on my bed with me," Bayly said. "Even if it is red with a fur coat."

SLIM PICKINGS

DISPATCHER: 911, may I help you?

CALLER: Is this animal control?

DISPATCHER: We dispatch animal control officers too. What can I help you with?

CALLER: Well, I need someone to come out right away to remove a dead squirrel from my backyard. You see, the crows are picking it all apart and throwing it all over my yard!

A GOOD NEIGHBOR POLICY

DISPATCHER: 911, can I help you?

MAN: I hope so. This is the third night in a row we've had to report the crime of disturbing the peace against the same person at the same address.

DISPATCHER: Okay.

MAN: And they have an alarm that keeps going off all night long. *On and off, on and off, and it's driving us crazy, we can't sleep. Will you please put them under arrest . . . please! Thank you!*

DISPATCHER: Hello? Hello?

I WOULDN'T BANK
ON HIS INTELLIGENCE

Larry Shelton James of Durham, North Carolina, waited until the cover of darkness to begin his nefarious plot. As he stood outside the First Union National Bank he knew what he wanted—all the money the bank had. His plan was simple— and apparently, so was he. James picked up a big rock and smashed the thick window next to the night deposit slot and crawled in. He landed on a desk and went about his cunning plan to steal the bank's money. As quick as a cat he prowled through the teller's drawers. Surely that's where they keep the money, he must have thought to himself. Nope, no money there. He turned his attention to the huge vault, but he didn't have a rock big enough to open it. Now for his escape. But wait! The doors were locked and there was glass all over the place near the window. If he crawled through he would surely cut himself to ribbons. What to do?

"He called 911 and said he got in and couldn't get out. He wanted the police to come and get him out," said Durham Police Sergeant M. C. Supples. Dispatchers kept the man on the line until the police arrived.

"I've never had an experience like that," Supples said. "When I got there, I saw a three-foot by three-foot hole in a window by the night deposit. There was glass all over the parking lot." Officers used their metal flashlights to smash the remaining glass and ordered James to exit the building the way he had entered. "He was real cooperative," Supples said. "I think he just wanted some help and didn't know how to get it or couldn't get it." I'll bet James didn't realize when he deposited himself in the bank he'd get a substantial penalty for an unsuccessful withdrawal.

-- 911 REPORT --

"Can an officer give me a ticket if he is not in uniform?
He was driving a police car and all,
but not in uniform, so does that count?"

AN IMAGINATION
IN LIVING COLOR

DISPATCHER: 911.

WOMAN: I'm going to want an ambulance . . .

DISPATCHER: What's the address, ma'am?

WOMAN: 1634 . . . not right now. Not now. Because it has to . . . the timing has to be right.

DISPATCHER: Ma'am, you're going to have to call when you need him. I can't schedule an officer.

WOMAN: Well, send a black one and a white one and a red one and a green one and one with a mustache and one with a beard and one with a red bandanna. Okay?

DISPATCHER: What's that for?

WOMAN: For props. Uh, for the nat . . . the television. For the color.

DISPATCHER: What for?

WOMAN: For national coverage.

DISPATCHER: Uh-huh. Okay.

WOMAN: Okay, thank you. I love you.

DISPATCHER: Good-bye.

BUT HE'S GOT HIGH HOPES, HE'S GOT HIGH HOPES, HE'S GOT . . .

DISPATCHER: 911. What is your emergency?

MALE CALLER: I need to report an animal bite.

DISPATCHER: Okay. Are you the one that was bitten?

MALE CALLER: No. It was my daughter that was bitten.

DISPATCHER: When did this happen?

MALE CALLER: It happened this afternoon.

DISPATCHER: Does your daughter need medical attention? Is she injured?

MALE CALLER: No. She is okay. She just has some scratches and a little bite mark. [snicker]

DISPATCHER: What was your daughter bitten by?

MALE CALLER: She was bitten . . . . She was bitten . . . [laughing] bitten by an anteater. [burst of laughter; in the background there is a slapping sound]

DISPATCHER: [trying not to laugh] A what?

MALE CALLER: An anteater. [laughing harder; slapping sound returns. (It is the daughter, who is a little upset about the father's sense of humor at the moment.)]

DISPATCHER: [laughing] Okay, okay. [laughing] I have to ask this next question. [laughing] Where in the world did your daughter encounter an anteater here in Virginia?

MALE CALLER: [regaining control] She and her mother were at a pet-a-pet farm in Winchester.

DISPATCHER: Oh, um. Okay. At least it makes some sense now. But now the bad news: That is outside of my jurisdiction so you will need to contact the local jurisdiction for that area.

MALE CALLER: Does that mean I have to tell this story again?

DISPATCHER: Yes, it does.

MALE CALLER: Bummer. [laughing] You would not happen to have the phone number for who I need to call, would you?

DISPATCHER: Not sure. I will check. Nope. I don't have their phone number, but I do have the number of the jurisdiction that borders Winchester. So give them a call and ask them for the phone number.

MALE CALLER: [laughing again] Okay. Thanks for the help.

DISPATCHER: You're welcome. And do yourself a favor, if I can suggest, don't tell them why you need the number. Just ask them for the number. [laughing]

MALE CALLER: Good idea.

NOTE: After this call was over, the concept of being bitten by an anteater became a puzzle to the Dispatcher. How can an animal with a long, tubelike nose designed for sucking insects out of holes or small cracks, open its mouth wide enough to bite a human? After a simple check in the dictionary the dispatcher also discovered that an anteater doesn't have teeth and therefore couldn't possibly have been the animal responsible for the bite. Could it have been a really ugly dog with a big nose?

WE'LL BE THERE IN A JIF

DISPATCHER: 911, fire or emergency?

MALE CALLER: It's an emergency.

DISPATCHER: Do you need a paramedic?

MALE CALLER: Yeah, I had a seizure and smacked my head on the kitchen counter.

DISPATCHER: Did you lose consciousness?

MALE CALLER: I don't think so. But I'm afraid I'll have another seizure and I'm just too weak to deal with it.

DISPATCHER: Sir, do you take medication for your seizures?

MALE CALLER: Yes, I take peanut butter balls.

DISPATCHER: Excuse me?

MALE CALLER: The doctor gave me a prescription for peanut butter balls.

DISPATCHER: Sir, do you mean phenobarbital?

MALE CALLER: Yeah. That would make more sense, wouldn't it?

PLEASE HANG UP
AND TRY AGAIN

It was a 911 hang-up and police officers were dispatched to a bank of pay phones in the parking lot outside Campie's Ice Cream store near Philadelphia. Officers Joseph Bryant and Christopher Crabtree saw two men hanging around the pay phones and noticed the phones had been damaged in an attempt to pry open the coin boxes. Apparently, when the two men, Alton S. Dotson and Marc Washington, were banging on the pay phones with a hammer, they accidentally dialed 911 on themselves. Bail on Dotson was set at $2,500. Washington was held on $5,500 bail. If these two guys paid their bail in quarters, police would surely know they had the right men.

-- 911 REPORT --

"What does it mean when your penis
shrinks and turns bright red?"

THREE STRIKES AND YOU'RE OUT

Police Officer Pete Renje of Oakland Park, Florida, was dispatched by a 911 operator to check on what could possibly be a child playing with the phone. Operators said they called the number but got no answer and on the second call got only the answering machine. Renje was about to summon a locksmith to the residence when he looked through the window and found the mystery caller—Jenny, a miniature dachshund puppy. "[The dog] gets up there and dances around the table and hits that little space bar and dials 911," Renje said. Before Renje had this all figured out Jenny had called the 911 number two more times, once using the handset, and the other time using the speaker-phone feature. When Jenny's owner, Chris Dolan, returned home, he found a note from the police officer asking him to either move the phone or move the dog. Dolan, who only had had the puppy for a week, wasn't too surprised about Jenny's phone fascination. The day before the puppy had recorded herself on the answering machine.

-- 911 REPORT --

Person reading the license plate number of a vehicle:
"U as in university, M as in New Mexico, and N as in knife."

LONG DISTANCE DISTRESS

This call was received in Monterey County, California, about three hundred miles north of Los Angeles.

DISPATCHER: 911 emergency, what are you reporting?

MALE CALLER: I want to report a hit-and-run accident.

DISPATCHER: Is anyone injured?

MALE CALLER: No.

DISPATCHER: Are you involved?

MALE CALLER: No, it's my girlfriend. She called me and I'm reporting it for her.

DISPATCHER: Where's your girlfriend?

MALE CALLER: She's on the 405.

DISPATCHER: She's on the 405? In Los Angeles?

MALE CALLER: Yes, she called me on her cell phone because she didn't know what to do. I'm calling for her.

DISPATCHER: Well, sir, this is Monterey County—about three hundred miles north of Los Angeles. We don't dispatch for that area. Can you call her back on her phone?

MALE CALLER: Sure.

DISPATCHER: Tell her to dial 911 on her own phone, and she'll get the people who can help her down there.

MALE CALLER: Okay, thanks.

THE PHANTOM OF 911

The night clerk at the Paso Robles Inn in California sits quietly behind the desk doing paperwork and getting things in order. Then the call comes. It usually rings in around 9:30 and it's always Room 1007. One would think it's an obnoxious guest calling for room service or someone looking for more towels, but it's—no one. The calls come in several times during the month and every time a staff member goes up to 1007 to investigate, the room is vacant. But when the nonentity in room 1007 called 911, the situation became really spooky. "That's not a glitch," said general manager Paul Wallace. In order to call an outside line one (or no one) would have to dial 8 and 0 before 911.

The general manager became curious and did a little investigating on his own. The hairs on his neck stood up when he came across an article in the *San Francisco Examiner* about the 1940 fire that had destroyed the original hotel. Wallace thought he discovered the phantom phoner—deceased night clerk J. H. Emsley. On December 19, 1940, Emsley discovered a fire raging on the second floor of the hotel. He hurried downstairs and sounded the alarm—then he clutched his left arm and died of a heart attack on the spot. "He had no idea that the two hundred guests were escorted out safely," Wallace theorizes; Emsley still thinks people are in danger—that's why he makes the calls.

A technician from Pacific Bell found nothing wrong with the hotel's phone line. Wallace even called a contractor to inspect the inside phone system. It worked perfectly. But here's the heavenly question: If the original hotel burned to the ground and a new one was built in its place, why would the ghost still be occupying the hotel? Wallace discovered the façade of the new hotel was built with bricks from—that's right—the old hotel.

-- 911 REPORT --

"Yeah, there's a moose running around out here with an Easter basket stuck around his neck."

A COCK-AND-BULL STORY

DISPATCHER: 911.

WOMAN: Hi, I would like to make a report.

DISPATCHER: Okay, about what?

WOMAN: Um, while walking to my car I saw a silver truck. Um, there was a young man in there . . . he was flicking his penis off.

DISPATCHER: How long ago was this?

WOMAN: This was just five minutes ago.

DISPATCHER: Okay, he was masturbating, then?

WOMAN: He was just flicking his *&#^ out of the window. My car was—

DISPATCHER: I'm sorry, he was . . . flicking?

WOMAN: He was, like, swinging his &%$% everywhere.

DISPATCHER: Okay. Okay. Like, he was swinging it out the . . . front window?

WOMAN: Yes. The driver window.

DISPATCHER: Okay. What did he look like?

WOMAN: Well, he was lying down, so I don't know. All I saw was his—was his penis swinging around.

DISPATCHER: That's weird. Okay.

WOMAN: I just want to protect other people, that's all.

DISPATCHER: All right, thank you.

WOMAN: Bye-bye.

[Dispatcher calls police]

DISPATCHER: 25 Fox-trot, check for a 314 vehicle.

POLICE: 25 Fox-trot [unintelligible].

DISPATCHER: 25 Fox-trot. [unintelligible] stated it was a male suspect. No actual description on him. He was in a newer, silver, medium-size truck. He was . . . at times . . . 10-23. [long pause] Suspect mostly lying down in the vehicle but he does swing his penis out the window.

POLICE: [laughing] 25 copy.

A ROSE BY ANY OTHER NAME . . .

DISPATCHER: 911, where is your emergency?

MALE CALLER: Can't I speak to a detective there, Detective Booreaoo?

DISPATCHER: Who, sir?

MALE CALLER: Detective Booreaoo, I think.

DISPATCHER: Can you spell it, please?

MALE CALLER: Sure, B-U-R-E-A-U.

DISPATCHER: Detective Bureau? Sir, that isn't a man's name.

MALE CALLER: Oh, it's a woman?

DISPATCHER: No, it's a place, sir. Hold on, I'll transfer you . . .

INSTANT JUSTICE

Linda Martinez, a twenty-year-old woman from Tucson, Arizona, was angry with the police for arresting her on vandalism charges. And to prove how unsubstantiated the charges were, she set about slashing twenty-four tires on six police cars parked outside the police station. On the last tire the knife slipped a little and Martinez cut a huge gash in her hand. "She cut her hands with the butcher knife she used to slash the tires and called 911," said an unidentified police officer. "This gets dumber. She told the operator she cut her hands while slashing 'the tires on your [expletive] cars.'" Paramedics treated Martinez at the scene of the tire slashing. She was arrested after the treatment but released on her own recognizance. In this case the wheels of justice turned quickly.

-- 911 REPORT --

"Yes, this is the 7-Eleven. I want to report some juveniles sucking on the Slurpee machine."

STEALING THE SHIRT
OFF YOUR BACK

DISPATCHER: 911.

WOMAN: Yeah, I don't know if I need, like, *emergency* emergency, but who do I talk to if someone just walked off with all your laundry at the Laundromat?

DISPATCHER: Call [gives local police number].

WOMAN: Thanks.

DIFFERENCE IN AGES

DISPATCHER: Do you need police or paramedics?

CALLER: Yes.

DISPATCHER: What is your emergency?

CALLER: Well, um, I'm three weeks pregnant, and, um, I don't know.

DISPATCHER: How old are you?

CALLER: Um . . . let's see . . . I'll be thirty-five, um, next year, I think.

DISPATCHER: No, how old are you *now*?

CALLER: Thirty-two.

THIS JOB IS FOR THE BIRDS

Several calls came into the emergency communications center in McMinnville, Tennessee, at the same time. Numerous traffic accidents had occurred at approximately the same time. "Someone called 911 and said there was a big chicken running down the middle of the highway, dividing traffic right and left," said Warren County Humane Society President Paul Mahar. The caller wasn't cuckoo—it was a bird all right, but not a chicken. It was a muscular, six-foot emu that had caused all the confusion. Darting in and out of traffic, the daring big bird rubber-necked so many drivers that several of them crashed into each other on U.S. 70 South.

The Humane Society was dispatched, but before they could arrive five Warren County sheriff's deputies and three civilian bystanders tried to trap the cagey bird. "They finally got him down, but he broke loose. Then they got some steel wire and managed to tie him up."

The bird had his feathers ruffled, and the arresting officers sustained scratches, cuts, bruises, and a peck or two. Finally, the emu was plucked from the scene and carted off to the Humane Society's animal shelter. But where to put the enormous emu? They were forced to lock him up in the only place they had available—a cell right next to the cats. "Thirty-seven cats had the hair on their backs standing straight up the whole day until they could get the emu out of there," Mahar said. I'll bet several of those cats' nine lives were scared out of them that day.

THE DEVIL MADE HIM DO IT

OPERATOR: 911.

CALLER: Hi, is this 911?

OPERATOR: Yes, this is 911. What is your emergency?

CALLER: Uh, my boyfriend, like, got this new tattoo a few days ago and it's, like, making him act weird.

OPERATOR: I see. In what way is he acting weird?

CALLER: I don't know. He just doesn't seem to be normal. He does weird stuff, you know?

OPERATOR: Could you give me a specific example, ma'am?

CALLER: Well, like yesterday he found a toad in the bushes and he brought it inside and started chanting over it.

OPERATOR: I see. Did he do anything else with the toad?

CALLER: Yeah, it was really gross. He like crucified it.

OPERATOR: I see. This tattoo, ma'am, is it some sort of Satanic symbol?

CALLER: I'm not sure.

OPERATOR: Is it an upside-down cross, or the number 666, or a five-pointed star?

CALLER: No, it's like some kind of goat with funny twisted horns.

OPERATOR: Okay. Ma'am, where do you live?

CALLER: In an apartment.

OPERATOR: No, I mean what is your address?

CALLER: Oh. I'm not sure. We live in this house right next door to, like, this church out on Tenth Street.

OPERATOR: You live next door to a church?

CALLER: Yeah, it's, like, a Baptist church or something.

OPERATOR: Does your boyfriend live there too?

CALLER: Well, sort of. He actually lives with his parents, but he stays with me most of the time.

OPERATOR: I see. Is he there now?

CALLER: No, he's, like, out drinking with his friends.

OPERATOR: Do you expect him back soon?

CALLER: I don't know. I don't think so.

OPERATOR: Okay. Do you have anyone you can stay with tonight?

CALLER: Why? Is he, like, contagious or something?

OPERATOR: No, but he could be dangerous, ma'am.

CALLER: Oh. Is he, like, crazy or something?

OPERATOR: There's no telling what he might do, ma'am. He has become a minion of Satan.

CALLER: Oh my God. Oh my God.

OPERATOR: Please try to remain calm, ma'am. Is there anyone you can stay with until your boyfriend can get proper treatment?

CALLER: [crying] I guess I could stay with my old boyfriend for a while.

OPERATOR: Does he have any tattoos?

CALLER: Yeah. Like, I mean, who doesn't?

OPERATOR: Can you describe them to me?

CALLER: Well, he's got a big dragon on his back. And a heart with a knife through it on his arm. And he's got one of those little naked mermaid kind of things on his, you know, his penis.

OPERATOR: Is that all?

CALLER: Yeah, I'm pretty sure.

OPERATOR: Okay. He should be safe. You should see if you can stay with him for a while. Will you do that?

CALLER: Yeah. Is my boyfriend going to be all right?

OPERATOR: I'm afraid he is damned for all eternity. But we need to think about you now, right? And make sure you're safe.

CALLER: [crying] Oh my God. I can't believe this is happening to us.

REPORT . . . 911 REPORT . . . 911 REP

. 911 REPORT . . . 911 REPORT . . . 91

RT . . . 911 REPORT . . . 911 REPORT

. 911 REPORT . . . 911 REPORT . . . 91

REPORT . . . 911 REPORT . . . 911 REP

. 911 REPORT . . . 911 REPORT . . . 91

REPORT . . . 911 REPORT . . . 911 REP

. 911 REPORT . . . 911 REPORT . . . 91

"Is the unemployment office open?"

REPORT . . . 911 REPORT . . . 911 REP

. 911 REPORT . . . 911 REPORT . . . 91

REPORT . . . 911 REPORT . . . 911 REP

. 911 REPORT . . . 911 REPORT . . . 91

REPORT . . . 911 REPORT . . . 911 REP

. 911 REPORT . . . 911 REPORT . . . 91

REPORT . . . 911 REPORT . . . 911 REP

CRYING WOLF

Police In Toronto, Canada, finally traced down a notorious 911 prankster who placed more than three hundred calls in two weeks. According to Sergeant Ray Price, "The crank calls ranged from ordering a pizza to a call alleging her grandmother was dying in front of her." She also called to tell the operator people had fallen and needed medical attention. But police soon found it was the girl herself who needed the attention. An eleven-year-old girl, living with her grandmother, turned out to be the cell phone culprit. Making harassing phone calls carries a maximum fine of $2,000, but the girl is too young to be charged with the offense. The girl's actions are out of the hands of the police but now into the hands of her grandparents, who were "suitably upset," according to Price. Now there's a good chance her next call to 911 will be a real one.

AND ONE FOR THE ROAD

DISPATCHER: Police emergency.

WOMAN: This isn't really an emergency, but it is sort of one to this little old lady. I've been terribly upset and I thought the only thing I could do, I don't think of sleeping pills and all of that, I went out and bought myself a couple of small bottles of beer. I thought that might relax me.

DISPATCHER: What's the problem?

WOMAN: The problem is I can't open the bottle. Could you send a man over and I'll be downstairs and have him open the bottle.

DISPATCHER: Okay, now wait a minute, okay, wait a minute. Am I correct that you can't sleep so you went out and bought two bottles of beer and you want a policeman to come by and open them for you?

WOMAN: Yes, please. Because I don't have any equipment here that seems to handle that kind of a top. And uh, I've never gone in . . . I think I had a ketchup bottle once and the neighbor broke the top off.

DISPATCHER: Ahhh. Well, listen, I'm going to get someone out there to open those beer bottles. You just stay in your apartment, ma'am, and I'll send him up to the apartment. What's your phone number?

WOMAN: Uh . . . wait until I take a look at it. It's a new one and I don't remember it very well. Oh, what the hell, I can hardly see it. It's all blotted and blurred it looks like. I can't see it without a magnifier . . .

DISPATCHER: Okay, you can't see it without a magnifying glass. That's okay that I don't know your phone number now.

WOMAN: Well, it looks like it. It has been put in by the operator or the one that put the phone in. And it's down below and that was it and then they put another one on top and now they're sort of over-blurred. I'm sorry about that . . .

DISPATCHER: Ohhhh, that's okay. I'll just get . . .

WOMAN: I'm, I'm cold sober, and . . .

DISPATCHER: I know you are . . .

WOMAN: Yeah, and I don't have any bad intent or anything. I just want to be able to go to sleep.

DISPATCHER: I know. Well, we're going to get you someone out there to open that beer bottle.

WOMAN: Thank you. You're lovely, dear.

DISPATCHER: You're welcome.

WOMAN: Should I hang up?

DISPATCHER: Yes.

WOMAN: Okay.

DISPATCHER: Bye-bye.

WOMAN: Bye-bye.

[Dispatcher calls police]

DISPATCHER: Q-affirmative.

POLICE: Security calling.

DISPATCHER: Q-affirmative. Assist the elderly female.

POLICE: Assist her to do what?

DISPATCHER: Uh, Charlie Q, it's been okay per the lieutenant, we prefer not to give the code out over the air.

THIS GIRL WASN'T ALL THUMBS

The 911 communications dispatch center in Gaston County, North Carolina, lit up with eight callers all notifying the police there was a woman hitchhiking on Interstate 85. Obviously not a life-or-death situation, but from the description of the woman the dispatchers realized they were looking at the potential for major traffic accidents. Why? Well, the woman, forty-three-year-old Hamza Schwenking-Ben, from Nuremberg, Germany, was hitchhiking from Georgia to Virginia with more than her thumb sticking out. In fact, everything was sticking out. She was hitchhiking in the nude. The defrocked femme fatale was unsuccessful in getting a ride but she did get motorists' attention. She also got the attention of a state trooper, who placed her under arrest (and under wraps).

-- 911 REPORT --

"The front canopy of my mobile home has a lot of snow weighing it down. What do I do?"

I'M TRYING TO REACH
MR. FISHER PRICE

DISPATCHER: 911 emergency, what are you reporting?

SMALL BOY: [startled gasp] I thought this was a *toy phone!*

DISPATCHER: No, you've reached 911—do you have an emergency?

SMALL BOY: [crying] Nooo! I was just playing! I'm sorry!

DISPATCHER: Is your mom or dad there?

SMALL BOY: I was *just playing!*

DISPATCHER: Let me talk to your dad.

[Adult male voice gets on the line]

FATHER: Hello?

DISPATCHER: This is 911. Is there an emergency there?

FATHER: Oh, no. My son . . . he thought this was a toy.

DISPATCHER: Well, sir, he got 911. We have to check out all these calls. Could you disable your one-button 911 speed-dial, or lock the keypad, so it doesn't happen again?

FATHER: Uhhh. Sure . . . it's just a cell phone, though.

DISPATCHER: Well, we answer 911 on cell phones *too*, sir.

FATHER: I guess you're right, sure.

A MINOR MISTAKE

DISPATCHER: 911, what is the emergency?

WOMAN: Yes, can you tell me how many months before your birthday are you legally twenty-one?

DISPATCHER: You are legally twenty-one *on* your birthday ma'am.

WOMAN: Oh, I thought it was the day before.

ATTACKER ON THE PROWL

"He just grabbed my legs," said eighty-three-year-old Edna Brown of her attacker. "I pulled him off and I threw him into the corner and then he went and attacked me again. He wouldn't let go," she said, reliving the horror of her experience. Volunteer firefighters were dispatched from a 911 operator and entered the premises looking for the attacker. "When we arrived there was lots of blood in the hallway, up the walls, and on the door," said Kieran Kelly, one of four firefighters. While Edna Brown was safe at the neighbor's house having her wounds tended to, firefighters slowly searched her house looking for the crazed attacker. Then they spotted him— crouching in the corner, blood on his face. It was McGuinty, Brown's eleven-year-old pussycat. "This thing was vicious. It was quite an episode. The cat was hissing and showing its teeth. We finally caught it in a fish net," said Dale Martin, deputy chief of the fire department.

The cat was taken to a local vet to be checked for diseases and to discover why the usually contented cat cracked and attacked.

-- 911 REPORT --

"I'm going to kill myself if you don't get the power turned back on. My sixty parrots will die!"

I DON'T NEED 911, I NEED 911

DISPATCHER: 911, what's the address of your emergency?

CITIZEN: Yes, I need the number that someone would dial for a medical or fire emergency other than 911.

DISPATCHER: We would like you to call 911 for those types of calls.

CITIZEN: No, I need the phone number for the dispatcher I would call in the case of a fire or medical emergency . . .

GOOD CITIZEN—SIT, STAY

DISPATCHER: 911, what's the address of your emergency?

CITIZEN: I am at the light at 100 South 100W, and the light has not changed, and I cannot cross the street. I am on foot and I have been here about fifteen minutes. Can you send an officer to make the light change? I can't cross against the light because I don't want to get arrested for breaking the law.

GOOD THINGS DON'T ALWAYS COME IN SMALL PACKAGES

There have been a number of stories regarding burglars who've broken into stores and called 911 because they couldn't get out. You'd have to get up pretty early to make another story like that interesting, but in this case, the subject has to go to bed early. He's only nine years old. In Bridgeport, Connecticut, a call came into the 911 center from a small boy who had hidden in the Factory Bedding & Furniture Outlet and stuffed his pockets with six hundred dollars in cash and forty-four packs of Pokémon cards. Soon realizing the owner locks the door after he leaves, the pint-size purloiner panicked and called 911. The boy was charged with criminal attempt to commit third-degree burglary, third-degree larceny, and second-degree criminal mischief. He was released into the custody of his great-grandmother and then sent to bed without supper.

REPORT . . . 911 REPORT . . . 911 REP
. 911 REPORT . . . 911 REPORT . . . 91
RT . . . 911 REPORT . . . 911 REPORT
. 911 REPORT . . . 911 REPORT . . . 91
REPORT . . . 911 REPORT . . . 911 REP
. 911 REPORT . . . 911 REPORT . . . 91

"You got to help
save my cat from
one really mean
raccoon."

REPORT . . . 911 REPORT . . . 911 REP
. 911 REPORT . . . 911 REPORT . . . 91
REPORT . . . 911 REPORT . . . 911 REP
. 911 REPORT . . . 911 REPORT . . . 91
REPORT . . . 911 REPORT . . . 911 REP
. 911 REPORT . . . 911 REPORT . . . 91
REPORT . . . 911 REPORT . . . 911 REP

OH WHERE, OH WHERE HAS MY LITTLE DOG GONE ...

DISPATCHER: 911.

WOMAN: Yes, Butchie is loose and I can't catch him.

DISPATCHER: Pardon me?

WOMAN: Ronald's dog is loose, Butchie. He told me to watch Butchie for him and Butchie got away from me.

DISPATCHER: Where is Butchie going?

WOMAN: He's on his leash. Would you guys please help me find Butchie before Ronald beats my butt.

DISPATCHER: No we can't, I'm sorry.

WOMAN: We've got to find Butchie.

DISPATCHER: Well, we can't help you on something like that because we're the police department and we have to handle burglars and criminals ...

WOMAN: But Butchie's gone!

DISPATCHER: Sorry.

WOMAN: Gosh. Butchie's gone!

DISPATCHER: You'll have to find Butchie yourself or get somebody else to help you find Butchie.

WOMAN: Gosh. Okay, thank you.

DISPATCHER: Okeydoke, good-bye.

YOU'D BE PARANOID TOO
IF EVERYONE WAS OUT TO GET YOU!

DISPATCHER: 911, what's the address of your emergency?

CITIZEN: Every time one of your undercover officers sees me, they spray me with pepper spray and try to arrest me. I have never done anything wrong in my life, but every time they see me they spray me. I need to find out how to stop that.

IT'S IN THE BAG

DISPATCHER: Dispatch.

MAN: Good morning.

DISPATCHER: Hi.

MAN: I'm a retired detective.

DISPATCHER: Okay.

MAN: Across the street from me there is, like, some-body trapped in a bag, or something.

DISPATCHER: A bag?

MAN: Yeah.

DISPATCHER: Is it on the lawn?

MAN: No, it is across from the garage. I'm looking at it right now but I can't figure it out.

DISPATCHER: Is it small?

MAN: No. Big.

DISPATCHER: A sleeping bag or a plastic bag?

MAN: Well, it looks like, uh, a bedsheet or something . . .

DISPATCHER: Okay, we'll be out in a minute. Thank you.

911 IS NOT A TOY

An emergency situation is a relative thing. To some it means the possible loss of life and limb. To a five-year-old girl, however, it could mean her yo-yo broke. And three days before Christmas 1999, that's just what happened to Emily Barg— that and the fact she was curious to see what would happen if she called 911. When the fire department showed up at her house, she realized what the call would bring—trouble. Little Emily was lectured on the dangers of what she had done and made to promise she would never call again unless it was a real emergency.

Emily showed up at the fire station a few hours later to apologize in the best way she knew how—with a plate of homemade chocolate chip cookies and a note that read: "I am very, very sorry. I baked these cookies for you. I hope you like them and you can forgive me. Now I am going to write a letter to Santa to tell him I am sorry, too."

The firefighters quickly accepted the little girl's apology and gobbled down all the cookies.

-- 911 REPORT --

"I have an elderly lady here who has been in an accident. She was riding on a shopping cart and fell off."

LIFE OR DEATH—YOU MEAN, I GET A CHOICE?

DISPATCHER: 911.

MAN: I'm dying.

DISPATCHER: Well, how do you know you're dying?

MAN: I have a strange premonition about death.

DISPATCHER: Have you taken any medication?

MAN: No.

DISPATCHER: And do you have any weapons on you?

MAN: No, of course not.

DISPATCHER: Have you had anything to drink tonight?

MAN: Oh, no, never would I have a drink.

DISPATCHER: Okay, well, I'm going to send the police out, but . . .

MAN: How nice of you. Finally! Get their asses out here, please!

DISPATCHER: Okay, sir?

MAN: Yeah?

DISPATCHER: I'm going to send the police out, but I need to know do you need an ambulance, also?

MAN:	The police are coming? When shall they be here?
DISPATCHER:	In a few minutes, but I need a—
MAN:	Yes, when they get here. You may speak with them.
DISPATCHER:	I may speak with who?
MAN:	The police.
DISPATCHER:	I don't need to speak with the police, sir, you do.
MAN:	Oh. [unintelligible]
DISPATCHER:	Okay, but I need to know, sir, you're saying that you're dying?
MAN:	Yes, I'm dying.
DISPATCHER:	Okay, I need to know if you need an ambulance and if so, they're going to ask—
MAN:	I don't know. I may just pass away.
DISPATCHER:	Okay. When I call the fire department for them to send an ambulance—
MAN:	[laughing] You called the fire department?
DISPATCHER:	Yeah, they're the ones who send the ambulance out. They're going to need to know why.
MAN:	Why?
DISPATCHER:	So I need to tell them.

MAN:	Why am I dying?
DISPATCHER:	Yes.
MAN:	I don't know. May I tell you where I'm located?
DISPATCHER:	Yes. Yes, that would be nice.
MAN:	Travel****
DISPATCHER:	Okay, are you in there alone?
MAN:	Of course, of course. Except for my three grandchildren.
DISPATCHER:	You have three—
MAN:	My cats, my three cats.
DISPATCHER:	Okay. You're the only human inside that room, is that correct?
MAN:	Yeah.
DISPATCHER:	Okay.
MAN:	And my cats are very dear to me. They are more important to me than my grandchildren.
DISPATCHER:	Okay, where are your grandchildren at?
MAN:	I don't know.
DISPATCHER:	Uh, okay. Why did you mention them then?
MAN:	Because uh, the cats are sort of substitutes for the grandchildren.

DISPATCHER: Okay, where do your grandchildren live?

MAN: They're here with me at Travel****.

DISPATCHER: They live with you at the Travel****?

MAN: Of course, of course. In the bathroom.

DISPATCHER: Okay. Where are they at right now?

MAN: In the bathroom.

DISPATCHER: So they are there?

MAN: They are here.

DISPATCHER: Okay. You told me that they weren't there—only the cats were there.

MAN: No, the cats are my grandchildren.

DISPATCHER: Ohhhhhh, okay! So you don't have any actual human grandchildren then?

MAN: Oh, no, no.

DISPATCHER: Oh, okay. Are you married?

MAN: No.

DISPATCHER: No. Okay, what's going on, though?

MAN: I don't know. I don't know. I'm dying.

DISPATCHER: Okay, but you don't know why you're dying?

MAN: No, I don't know why I'm dying.

[Knock at the door]

MAN: I hark! Hark! Would you excuse me, please?

DISPATCHER: Certainly.

MAN: May I call you back?

DISPATCHER: Why don't you just leave the phone line open?

MAN: Oh, of course. I'm leaving the phone line open. [to the officers at the door] Just a moment! Who is it?

[Dispatcher laughs]

MAN: The police are here.

DISPATCHER: Yeah, that's who you called, sir.

MAN: What?

DISPATCHER: That's who you called. Remember?

MAN: The police are here!

DISPATCHER: Right.

MAN: They may not cross the threshold.

DISPATCHER: They may not cross—

MAN: They may not cross the threshold, no.

DISPATCHER: Well, sir, you called, you said you were dying—

MAN: Yes.

DISPATCHER: And you needed help.

MAN: Yes—

DISPATCHER:	That's why I sent the police.
MAN:	Oh, look. [to the police] What? Close the door as you leave! [Back to the dispatcher on the phone] Hello?
DISPATCHER:	Yeah? Sir.
MAN:	Uh-huh.
DISPATCHER:	Okay, what is it you'd like us to help you with? You called 911 . . .
MAN:	Yes.
DISPATCHER:	Okay. You said you were dying.
MAN:	Yes.
DISPATCHER:	Okay. And so I sent you the police. Is there something else I can help you with?
MAN:	Yeah, uh, send the police back.
DISPATCHER:	Why?
MAN:	Send the paramedics.
DISPATCHER:	Okay, so you don't want the police, then.
MAN:	Oh, I do, I do, I do, I do.
DISPATCHER:	Well, why don't you go step outside and talk with them then?
MAN:	Oh, I will. Hold the line, please.
DISPATCHER:	Okay, go ahead.

911 REPORT ... 911 REPORT ... 911 REPORT
911 REPORT ... 911 REPORT ... 911 RE
... 911 REPORT ... 911 REPORT ...
911 REPORT ... 911 REPORT ... 911 RE
PORT ... 911 REPORT ... 911 REPORT
911 REPORT ... 911 REPORT ... 911 RE

"Yes, there is a house
in my neighborhood
that always parks on
the sidewalk."

911 REPORT ... 911 REPORT ... 911 RE
PORT ... 911 REPORT ... 911 REPORT
911 REPORT ... 911 REPORT ... 911 RE
PORT ... 911 REPORT ... 911 REPORT
911 REPORT ... 911 REPORT ... 911 RE
PORT ... 911 REPORT ... 911 REPORT

OUT FOR THE COUNT

"He's getting a real battering and blood is everywhere!" yelled a frightened woman to the 999 (Scotland's equivalent of 911) operator. The operator was prepared to dispatch the police when a few questions made it clear the assault the woman was referring to was on television. Sixty-four-year-old Nora Cuthbert was upset because her favorite wrestling icon, "Stone-Cold" Steve Austin, was getting a beating by "Triple H" in a World Wrestling Federation bout broadcast live from Manchester. The officer tried to explain to Ms. Cuthbert that her call was not an emergency and, besides, wrestling is all made up anyway. Ms Cuthbert wouldn't have any of that. She begged the officer to stop the match and save "Stone-Cold" before he became stone-dead. "People say it is not real and it is all staged, but I knew it was real and he was hurt and I wasn't going to stand by and watch it happen," said Ms. Cuthbert after the event. It's lucky that an officer never arrived at her house. It's rumored she keeps a metal folding chair on hand at all times.

&*^# OUT OF LUCK

DISPATCHER: 911, what's the address of your emergency?

CITIZEN: Yes, I need to know how to get my dog run cleaned out. I don't have time to do it myself.

DISPATCHER: Ma'am, this is 911, police emergency . . .

CITIZEN: And I also need to know what to do with all that dog poop when I am done.

THE PHONE IS ON THE SAME FREQUENCY AS MY MIND

DISPATCHER: 911, what's the address of your emergency?

CITIZEN: Yes, I'd like to report that I hear voices and see shadows, and I've been receiving threats lately.

DISPATCHER: Okay, sir, where exactly are these things happening?

CITIZEN: Well, I'm not sure they're even here in Utah. They travel through sound waves and TV signals.

A MOOOOVING VIOLATION

Several concerned citizens called the 911 center in Debary, Florida, to alert the police of a "drowning cow." The cow wasn't drowning, however; he was simply walking in knee-deep water in a flooded field. The calls were coming so frequently that highway workers set up an electronic sign that flashed the message THE COW IS OK. Putting the sign up was a good move; leaving the sign up for two days wasn't. People continued to slow down to look for the cow who was "OK" (a cow who, in fact, wasn't there anymore), and therefore caused traffic jams along the stretch of road for several days.

-- 911 REPORT --

"There is a snow sculpture outside my apartments,
gross exaggeration of certain male parts,
that we all find obscene."

IT KEEPS ON WORKING,
AND WORKING, AND WORKING . . .

DISPATCHER: 911, what's your emergency?

MAN: Yeah, it's a little unusual.

DISPATCHER: What's the problem, sir?

MAN: Well, I was just playing around and I got—uh, this is the honest truth, don't laugh—I put my girlfriend's vibrator, I got it up in there, and I can't get it out.

DISPATCHER: I'm sorry, I can't understand you, sir. Try again.

MAN: I was playing with my girlfriend's vibrator and I got it up in and I can't get it out. And that's the honest to God's truth.

DISPATCHER: I...I . . .

MAN: I've tried everything.

DISPATCHER: I'm sorry, I just can't understand what you're saying to me. You've got your girlfriend's what?

MAN: Her vibrator.

DISPATCHER: Okay.

MAN: I was playing with it. It was stupid, but I got it up and I can't get it out. I've tried everything.

DISPATCHER: Okay, sir, I can get a medic out there to help you.

MAN: Okay.

COME ON BACK NOW, YA HEAR?

A call came into the emergency communications center in Dickson, Tennessee, from a man whose wife was having difficulty breathing. An ambulance was dispatched and arrived at the small trailer park to find the husband sitting on the stoop drinking a beer. The paramedics entered the trailer and found the young woman sitting on the sofa obviously not in distress. They began to take her vital signs and asked her to tell them her problem. She told the paramedics that she and her husband were having sex when all of a sudden her skin started tingling, her heart started racing, her muscles tightened up and she had shortness of breath. She said the problem only lasted a few seconds and then she felt flushed all over and wondered if she had suffered a seizure. The paramedics, trying to keep from laughing, told the woman she probably just had her first orgasm, but would she like to go to the hospital just in case? "No," she chirped. "I don't want to go to the hospital. I want another one of those."

WHOSE BRIGHT IDEA WAS THIS?

During a power outage in southern Florida, numerous calls came into the 911 communications center. Many people complained about being without power, others asking when their power would be restored, calls, of course, that shouldn't have been made. Here's an example:

DISPATCHER: 911, fire or emergency.

MALE CALLER: My power's out!

DISPATCHER: Yes, sir, we're aware of that. Do you have an emergency?

MALE CALLER: No, I don't have a damn emergency. I just want to know if I'm going to be getting a rebate for the length of time I'm without power?

DISPATCHER: Uhhhhh, no, sir, you won't be charged for the electricity you *didn't* use . . . .

MALE CALLER: Well, that's more like it!

YOU PICKED A FINE TIME
TO LEAVE ME, LOOSE WHEEL

DISPATCHER: 911, what's the address of your emergency?

CITIZEN: I need an officer to come and fix my bike. It is dangerous because the front wheel is not on tight. I am at work and there is nobody here to help me and I need to run some errands while the officer is working on the bike.

RENFIELD, QUICK, CALL 911

DISPATCHER: 911, what's the address of your emergency?

CITIZEN: Can you tell me what animal control does with the rats they pick up? I am looking for a large rat, about the size of a dog, to breed, and none of the rats in the pet stores are large enough!

EMERGENCY CALL TO MARTHA STEWART

A woman in Whitehall, Ohio, watched as her sixty-year-old husband died of a heart attack. The woman refused to call 911 for help fearing the police would discover her extremely cluttered house and arrest her.

-- 911 REPORT --

Fifty-three-year-old grandmother
wants police officer to run to the store
for the four kids she's baby-sitting.

THE CRIMINAL MIND—
AND OTHER OXYMORONS

Shawn Socha, who was on the lam after robbing a Marietta, Ohio, bank with his wife, was hiding out from the law in Huntington, West Virginia. He was curious if police had a clue to his whereabouts. So our incompetent criminal dialed 911 to see if there were any outstanding warrants against him. The operator simply traced the call and police picked up the clueless couple.

THE KEY TO HAPPINESS

DISPATCHER: 911, please state the nature of your emergency.

MAN: Yeah, I'm a little embarrassed but I've locked my keys in the car.

DISPATCHER: Sir, 911 is for life-and-death emergencies only.

MAN: Yeah, I'm real sorry about that, but I didn't know who else to call. I'm at a pay phone and I don't have any change.

DISPATCHER: Are there any infants or small children locked in the car, sir?

MAN: No, just my keys.

DISPATCHER: Is the car running?

MAN: Yeah, it runs great.

I SAID BREATHE FOR HER— NOT BREED WITH HER

DISPATCHER: 911, fire or emergency?

MALE CALLER: Emergency. Yeah, emergency.

DISPATCHER: What's the problem, sir?

MALE CALLER: It's my wife . . . oh, God, I don't think she's breathing.

DISPATCHER: Okay, the paramedics are on their way. Sir, do you know CPR?

MALE CALLER: Gosh, no. I don't no anything about that artificial insemination stuff.

SMOKE 'EM IF YOU GOT 'EM

A late-night call came into the otherwise quiet dispatch center. It was a heart patient with a question about one of his medications—the patch. He told the operator his cardiologist had recommended the nitroglycerin patch instead of the nitroglycerin pill. "So, what's the problem?" the dispatcher asked. "I'm running out of places to put them," he responded. Apparently the man had followed the directions and put on a new patch every six hours. He forgot, however, to remove the old ones. Paramedics helped the man take off the more than fifty patches that were covering his body. With that much nitroglycerin in his body it's a wonder he didn't explode.

REPORT . . . 911 REPORT . . . 911 REP
. 911 REPORT . . . 911 REPORT . . . 911
RT . . . 911 REPORT . . . 911 REPORT
. 911 REPORT . . . 911 REPORT . . . 911
REPORT . . . 911 REPORT . . . 911 REP
. 911 REPORT . . . 911 REPORT . . . 911
REPORT . . . 911 REPORT . . . 911 REP

"I smoked marijuana
an hour ago, and
now I feel dizzy."

REPORT . . . 911 REPORT . . . 911 REP
. 911 REPORT . . . 911 REPORT . . . 911
REPORT . . . 911 REPORT . . . 911 REP
. 911 REPORT . . . 911 REPORT . . . 911
REPORT . . . 911 REPORT . . . 911 REP
. 911 REPORT . . . 911 REPORT . . . 911
REPORT . . . 911 REPORT . . . 911 REP

DOGGONE IT!

After a hang-up call, the dispatcher calls back. A dog barks in the background.

WOMAN: Hello?

DISPATCHER: Yes, this is 911. We just got a hang-up call from this cell phone. Is there an emergency there?

WOMAN: You know what, it must have been hit when the dog stepped on it.

DISPATCHER: Okay, watch the phone, please.

THIS GUY IS NUTS!

DISPATCHER: Police emergency line.

MAN: Yes, uh, I have a person that, uh, needs service to a hospital.

DISPATCHER: Okay, do they need a paramedic?

MAN: [to the person] Do you need a paramedic?
No, he just needs to get to the hospital.

DISPATCHER: What's the problem with him?

MAN: [to the person] Uh, do you want to talk to her?

DISPATCHER: Yeah, let me talk to the person. Hello?

VICTIM: Okay. All right. I just got to go to the general hospital.

DISPATCHER: Okay. What's the problem?

VICTIM: Okay, uh, last night. Okay, I was sitting at the table, all right? And I got up and—excuse me for putting it this way—but my right nut, okay, it started hurting real bad.

DISPATCHER: Uh-huh.

VICTIM: Okay. And I've been going, you know, all day long today I've been walking around and right now it's inflamed about two times the size.

DISPATCHER: Can you go by paramedic?

VICTIM: I guess.

DISPATCHER: You're at the liquor store, right?

VICTIM: Yeah.

DISPATCHER: Okay. I'm going to call the paramedics. Now they'll probably call you back at this phone number, all right?

VICTIM: Okay.

DISPATCHER: While they're on the way they'll probably call you back.

VICTIM: All right.

DISPATCHER: Okay, bye-bye.

[Dispatcher calls paramedics.]

PARAMEDIC: Yo!

DISPATCHER: You're not going to believe this.

PARAMEDIC: Uh-oh. What is it?

DISPATCHER: I don't know how to tell you this. I've got this guy, he's at the liquor store, there. And he has an inflamed testicle and he can't walk and he would like the paramedics. And I put it to you a lot better than he put it to me.

PARAMEDIC: I can imagine, I can imagine.

DISPATCHER: I guess that's really painful, I don't know.

PARAMEDIC: I'll give him a ring.

DISPATCHER: Thank you, bye-bye.

PARAMEDIC: Bye-bye.

DOG DAY AFTERNOON

An operator in North Bay, Ontario, picked up the line when the caller dialed 0. There was no one on the other end of the line, but the operator felt something was wrong, so she transferred the call to the 911 communications center. The dispatcher recognized the sounds emanating from the phone as that of a dog in distress. The call was quickly traced back to its origin and a policeman was dispatched. When the officer arrived at the residence he could hear the panic-stricken dog from outside the house. The door was locked and no one was home, but the officer knew the dog needed immediate attention. So he climbed in through a narrow window, accidentally breaking the glass and cutting his arm. The caller, an eight-week-old puppy named Lacy, was choking on the telephone cord. The dog was immediately released and graciously licked the officer's face in thanks. The dog was fine, but the officer had to be taken to a local hospital and have nine stitches in his arm from the cut. Every dog has his day and, thanks to the fast actions of the dispatcher and the police officer, this dog will have many more days.

DISPATCHER SCREW-UPS:

●kay, this book is mostly about intellectually naive people calling 911 for stupid and frivolous reasons—but are the dispatchers always perfect? Uh, no. These reports were gathered by a friend who works at a 911 Communications Center—and all the names have been changed to protect the ignorant.

CITIZEN: My daughter is suicidal, and I think I need to report this.

DISPATCHER: Okay, ma'am. Has she ever committed suicide before?

DISPATCHER: Thank you for helping, can I hold you?

CALLER: I want to report a lewdness, a male exposed himself to me.

DISPATCHER: Okay, how long was he? . . . I mean, how long ago was that?

DISPATCHER: 3121, respond on a lewdness, totally naked white male. [gives address]

3121:   Could I get a description on the male?

DISPATCHER: Totally naked, white male.

Rescue 14 is sent out on a call. There is one victim of assault and the other is a victim of the officer's pepper spray. Rescue 19 comes over the radio and says, "R14, confirming you are responding on assault and pepper?"

GIVE HIM THE CHAIR

DISPATCHER: 911, what's the address of your emergency?

CITIZEN: I'd like to report a suicide at the Hotel Roberts.

DISPATCHER: Have they already done something, or are they just contemplating suicide?

CITIZEN: I threw some chairs out the window.

DISPATCHER: What does chairs out the window have to do with a suicide?

STOP FLAPPING YOUR LIPS

A Boston man, Cator Lewis-Charles, thirty-six, dialed 911 after he and his wife had gotten into a heated argument about a party he wanted to attend. The man grabbed his wife and then bit off her lower lip. Paramedics rushed the wife and the lip to the hospital, where the lip was reattached. The man was sentenced to five years of probation and the couple continue to live together with their two sons. Makes you wonder how they kissed and made up, doesn't it?

-- 911 REPORT --

"I think my swimming pool is going to freeze
and crack and flood my neighbors below.
It's made of a nonfreezing rubber liner."

HIS TESTICLE IS THE BOMB

DISPATCHER: 911.

WOMAN: I'm looking for, not the local police, uh, what's the name of your group down there, please? I'm not being arrogant, I'm calling from Ontario.

DISPATCHER: What are you trying to find out?

WOMAN: It's not the RCMP, it's, uh, I have a very important call to make because I just realized that my own son could be carrying a cobalt bomb in his testicle.

DISPATCHER: Who are you needing to contact, ma'am?

WOMAN: Pardon?

DISPATCHER: Who are you needing to contact?

WOMAN: Your head, head, head office. Your head police.

DISPATCHER: This is it, ma'am.

WOMAN: Yeah. Okay, thank you. He just came back to Canada in July and I believe he's carrying a cobalt bomb in his left testicle. And the stupid police don't know nothing. They won't even arrest him. And he could blow the planet so sky-high it would be detected. But a testicle that's swollen up and keeps moving around. But I believe he's changing, he's holding a dangerous weapon inside his own body, okay? Not his rectum—they're his testicles.

DISPATCHER: Okay, thanks for calling.

911 REPORT ... 911 REPORT ... 911 REPORT
911 REPORT ... 911 REPORT ... 911 RE
... 911 REPORT ... 911 REPORT ...
911 REPORT ... 911 REPORT ... 911 RE
PORT ... 911 REPORT ... 911 REPORT
911 REPORT ... 911 REPORT ... 911 RE
PORT ... 911 REPORT ... 911 REPORT

"I need a shot
to help my sex life."

WE'RE EXPERIENCING
TECHNICAL DIFFICULTIES

In London, England, the equivalent of the American and
Canadian 911 system is the 999 system—which is supposed
to be used exclusively for police, emergency, or fire. But the
intellectually challenged know no geographical barriers, and
the English get stupid calls just like the rest of us. Case in
point: A call came into the Wolverhampton (central England)
999 center with a call for help. Paramedics arrived to find the
victim's family standing around the lifeless body of—their
television set. Paramedics told the family not to use the 999
system for their television again and not to give them static
about it.

FISHING FOR TROUBLE

DISPATCHER: 911.

[A male voice is heard swearing, saying things like, "I'll get you, you little @$)#$&#ers! Where the #@Q)$87 ARE you?"]

DISPATCHER: This is 911—do you have an emergency?

[No response, but the man is obviously slamming things around. There are bashing sounds, and more swearing, liberal use of the f-word.]

DISPATCHER: This is 911—sir! Sir? *Hello?* Sir?

[The dispatcher, concerned the man will find whomever he's looking for and harm them, keeps the line open and continues trying to get his attention. The dispatcher is unable to locate the origin of the call as it's coming from a cell phone. Eventually the man gets closer to the receiver and the dispatcher yells.]

DISPATCHER: *This is 911! Hello? Can you hear me?*

[The man picks up the phone and is extremely calm.]

MAN: Hello?

DISPATCHER: Sir, this is 911. Is everything okay there?

MAN: Yeah. Wow, 911?

DISPATCHER: Yes. What's going on there? Who were you yelling at?

MAN: Uhhhh. Ummm. Wow. I was going fishing this morning and I couldn't find my worms—I don't know where I put them. I was just looking for them.

THE PERSONAL TOUCH

DISPATCHER: 911, fire or emergency?

OLDER WOMAN: I'm sorry to bother you, dear.

DISPATCHER: What's the problem, ma'am?

OLDER WOMAN: My home health care nurse is late and my back is hurting.

DISPATCHER: Ma'am, do you have an emergency there?

OLDER WOMAN: It's just that I think I'm getting sores on my back. Could you have someone come out and help turn me over? I'm an invalid is the only reason I'm asking.

DISPATCHER: How long have you been bedridden?

OLDER WOMAN: [long pause] Excuse me?

DISPATCHER: How long have you been bedridden?

OLDER WOMAN: Well, if you must know, not for about twenty years . . . when my husband was alive.

FILM STAR FAUX PAW

When Kenosha County, Wisconsin, dispatcher Diane Chromik took the call all she could hear was heavy breathing. It turned out the call was made by Sophia Loren—but she couldn't talk. "All I could hear was panting and the phone being moved on the floor," Chromik said. Police were immediately dispatched while Chromik stayed on the line. "At first, all I could hear was more heavy breathing," Chromik said. Then, from the background, she heard a woman yell "Bad dog!" and the phone was disconnected. Chromik called back and spoke to Nancy Brady. "She [Chromik] said, 'Two squads are on the way to your house,'" Brady said. "I think I said, 'It was Sophia!'" It did turn out to be Sophia Loren who made the call—not Sophia Loren the famous Italian actress, but Sophia Loren the six-month-old Labrador puppy. Brady explained that when the phone rang she let voice mail answer it, and the beeping must have intrigued the puppy. The puppy pawed out 911 while chewing on the phone. "It gave everybody a nice break and a laugh," Chromik said. "It's nice to have a happy ending." It would have been a happier ending for the cops if it had been the real Sophia Loren!

-- 911 REPORT --

"I'm at a coin phone, and it says that 911 calls are free. Thanks."

A BAD FIRST DATE

DISPATCHER: 911 emergency.

MAN: Yes, I have, I had a blond woman, nude, in a white Mitsubishi and somebody stole her. Somebody put a gun to her and took her. She's a blond and she's, uh . . .

DISPATCHER: When did this happen, sir?

MAN: Uh, just a matter of . . . five minutes ago.

DISPATCHER: Okay. You're a family member?

MAN: Yes.

DISPATCHER: How old is this person?

MAN: Uh, she's forty-five. Somebody stole her.

DISPATCHER: What do you mean, somebody stole her, sir?

MAN: Somebody robbed her. Took her. Nude.

DISPATCHER: Okay . . .

MAN: Gone!

DISPATCHER: This is a forty-year-old lady who lives with you?

MAN: No, no, no. She's uh, yeah, forty years old, lives with me. Oh, she's supposed to live with me.

DISPATCHER: Okay. Now, was she in the car by herself, or was she taken—

MAN: By herself.

DISPATCHER: Then how was she stolen?

MAN: What?

DISPATCHER: How was she stolen if she was riding in the car by herself?

MAN: I don't know. I don't know. Who . . . I'm, I'm . . . armed robbery, I guess.

DISPATCHER: I'm sorry?

MAN: Armed robbery.

DISPATCHER: Armed robbery?

MAN: Yeah, armed robbery, I guess.

DISPATCHER: Did she steal something from you?

MAN: Huh?

DISPATCHER: Did she steal something from you?

MAN: No, no, no. No, no, no, no.

DISPATCHER: Okay, so what's missing is the lady . . .

MAN: The lady and her car . . .

DISPATCHER: And her car?

MAN: Yeah, and her car, Mitsubishi. Gone. White.

DISPATCHER: Okay, sir. Have you been drinking or anything?

MAN: Yes, I have.

DISPATCHER: Okay, what I'm getting from your story is that, you're telling me, that this lady was stolen?

MAN: Yes.

DISPATCHER: Okay, sir. That's really not possible.

MAN: Oh. Okay.

DISPATCHER: If she's driving in the car by herself and no one took her . . .

MAN: Oh, okay. She's sneaking out of here. Okay, okay?

DISPATCHER: Okay. Bye.

WHEN WHAT TO MY WONDERING
EYES SHOULD APPEAR . . .

It sounded like a call right out of Whoville. While driving
around with his family looking at Christmas lights a man
spotted something on a neighbor's rooftop. It was Santa. But
not your plastic Santa with a light in his belly—no, this Santa
was frantically waving and shouting. Was he wishing everyone
a merry Christmas? Nope. He was begging someone to help
him down. The passerby called 911 and the fire department
helped the stranded Santa. Apparently Jolly Old Saint Nick
wasn't so jolly after his ladder broke and he was stuck on the
rooftop, click, click, click. Staying out in the winter wonder-
land for five hours gave this deserted do-gooder a mild case of
frostbite on one toe. The paramedics soon realized that the
rosy red cheeks weren't part of the outfit, either.

ENEMA OUTAMA

A slightly panicked husband called 911 one night asking advice from the dispatcher regarding his wife's medical condition. He explained to the operator his wife had been experiencing abdominal pain for a week and their doctor had prescribed giving the woman an enema to help relieve any pressure. The operator listened patiently, continuing to ask questions to determine the root of the problem. The doctor told the man that if the initial enema didn't do the trick to buy a few more at their local store and administer those as the directions indicated. Finally the man said, "I've given her four enemas since we saw the doctor. She drank all of them but they're not doing any good. What should I do?" The operator, who was nearly convulsed with laugher, explained to the man the proper way to use the enema. To which the man, cupping the receiver in his hand, yelled to his wife, "Honey, you got to stick 'em up your butt!"

-- 911 REPORT --

"My neighbor has power and I don't. It's a conspiracy!"

NOT A PROPERLY STOLEN CAR

DISPATCHER: Police emergency line, Parker.

WOMAN: Uh, Parker, would you connect me with stolen cars, please.

DISPATCHER: You want to report your car stolen?

WOMAN: That's why I called.

DISPATCHER: This is the correct number.

WOMAN: Pardon me?

DISPATCHER: This is the correct number.

WOMAN: All righty, you're in charge. Where do we go from here?

DISPATCHER: You want to report your car stolen, right?

WOMAN: That's what I said three times, yes.

DISPATCHER: Okay. Do you have any idea who took your car? Or . . .

WOMAN: I have a strong suspicion. I'm not positive.

DISPATCHER: Okay. When was the last time you saw your car?

WOMAN: About a week ago, perhaps a day or two more.

DISPATCHER: Did you loan it to anybody? Does anybody have keys to it?

WOMAN: No. There's a guest set of keys, but I have them.

DISPATCHER: Well, who is it you think has it?

WOMAN: Because I loaned it to him for an evening and he hasn't yet returned it.

DISPATCHER: Ahhhhh, so you don't want to report it stolen, you want to report your friend not returning it yet, correct?

WOMAN: I want the car. And as far as I'm concerned it is stolen . . .

DISPATCHER: No, it's—

WOMAN: . . . because he didn't have my permission to keep it for a week.

DISPATCHER: No, but you gave him permission to use it, so he didn't steal it. There's a difference between stealing and . . .

WOMAN: This is true, this is true. But what is the difference?

DISPATCHER: Well, he didn't steal it you gave it to him. You gave it to him . . .

WOMAN: No, no, no, honey, you're misinterpreting. I gave it to him for an evening.

DISPATCHER: Okay, but you're misinterpreting the word *steal*. He did not steal it.

WOMAN: All righty, well, think of the word we want to come up with.

DISPATCHER: He did not keep his end of the bargain.

WOMAN: This is true.

DISPATCHER: True. But he did not steal the car. He is keeping it past his deadline and he does need to give it back to you.

WOMAN: All right, now where do we go from there, dear?

DISPATCHER: I need you to call the auto theft detectives, tomorrow morning—

WOMAN: Hold on, hold on. God Almighty, what do you think I am, a machine? Tomorrow morning, call who?

DISPATCHER: The auto theft detectives.

WOMAN: Yeah. In other words there's nothing I can do until the morning?

DISPATCHER: Right.

WOMAN: Thank you so much.

DISPATCHER: You're very welcome.

WOMAN: You're very welcome, too.

THE HEAT IS ON

A young woman called the 911 center in Cleveland, Ohio, and complained to the operator that she wasn't feeling well and wished for an ambulance to take her to the hospital. The dispatcher went through several questions to ascertain the seriousness of the woman's condition. When she asked if the woman was running a fever the woman replied, "Yes, I just checked. It's seventy-two degrees." Now the normal human temperature is 98.6. A reading of seventy-two degrees is usually reserved for dead people and thawing chickens. The operator, thinking the woman had made a mistake, asked her to check her temperature again. The woman put down the phone and was back on the line in a matter of seconds. "I checked again," she said. "It's still seventy-two degrees." Since the check had only taken seconds, the operator wondered if the woman was using an ear thermometer. "What kind of thermometer are you using?" asked the befuddled dispatcher. "Oh, the one on the wall." Apparently, the woman had been checking the thermostat for her air conditioning unit.

-- 911 REPORT --

Woman complainant—neighbor's vibrator is too loud.

A VERY STICKY SITUATION

DISPATCHER: 911 emergency. What are you reporting?

MALE CALLER: Take this license plate down: [gives plate number].

DISPATCHER: [Repeats number while documenting it.] What are you reporting, sir?

MALE CALLER: I want that van stopped and the people arrested!

DISPATCHER: Where are you?

MALE CALLER: I'm following them—they threw gum out the window and it came in *my* open window!

DISPATCHER: Do you think they did it on purpose, sir?

MALE CALLER: Yes! It got in my son's hair! I'm not pulling over, I'm going to follow them until you get a cop here to stop them!

OUT FOR A SUNDAY DRIVE

DISPATCHER: 911, fire or emergency?

FEMALE CALLER: I'm intoxicated and I'm driving my car.

DISPATCHER: You say you're intoxicated and driving your car?

FEMALE CALLER: Yep.

DISPATCH: Ma'am, here's what I want you to do. I want you to pull over to the side of the road and turn the car off.

FEMALE CALLER: No, don't want to do that.

DISPATCHER: Ma'am, driving while intoxicated is extremely dangerous. You could hurt yourself or someone else. You don't want that, do you?

FEMALE CALLER: No, but I'm not pulling over. I'm driving.

DISPATCHER: Why don't you just pull over right now, ma'am, and I'll call you a taxi cab?

FEMALE CALLER: No, I don't want a taxi.

DISPATCHER: Ma'am, please understand the danger you're putting yourself and others in. Stop the car as soon as you can find a safe place. Please.

FEMALE CALLER: Nope.

DISPATCHER: Ma'am, if you're not going to take my advice, why did you call 911?

FEMALE CALLER: I don't know.

THE SEAT OF THE PROBLEM

Police dispatchers in Fayetteville, Arkansas, were wondering what all the hubbub was about at Razorback Stadium. They had received thirty-five emergency calls, but upon answering all they heard was the football game—no response from the caller. They knew the University of Arkansas had hog-tied the Middle Tennessee State Blue Raiders by 58 to 6—so it probably wasn't a call from the winning team. So why so many calls? Police soon found out the calls were coming from an overly excited Razorback fan who was constantly jumping up and down in his seat. Every time he sat down, his derriere dialed 911. So remember, folks, activate the keyguard on your phone or disconnect the one-button speed dial to 911. Together, we can eliminate accidental 911 calls one cheek at a time.

STOP CALLING ME!

DISPATCHER: 911, what's the address of your emergency?

CITIZEN: [No response]

DISPATCHER: 911, what's the address of your emergency?

CITIZEN: [tentatively] Hello?

DISPATCHER: Yes, this is 911, can I help you?

CITIZEN: You have the wrong number!

WHAT GOES UP
MUST COME DOWN

An obvious animal lover called the 911 center and asked if the fire department could come over and help get a squirrel off the top of a telephone pole. He complained that the poor creature had climbed up and now looked confused about how to get down. The dispatcher asked the man if he thought this was actually an emergency situation, and the man responded that it was for the stranded squirrel. Taking a deep breath, and trying not to laugh, the dispatcher asked the man a serious question. "Have you ever seen a squirrel skeleton on top of a telephone pole or even in a tree?" After a brief pause, the man quietly said no and apologized for calling.

-- 911 REPORT --

"I am calling to find out why an officer is calling me to do follow-up on an investigation on a *Sunday*?"

BARING FALSE WITNESS

A slightly intoxicated older woman called the 911 center in a small town in Wyoming asking for assistance in getting her false teeth out of the toilet. The woman explained she had had a little too much to drink and while she was throwing up, her teeth flew out of her mouth and went down the toilet. The dispatcher suggested the woman call a plumber, as lost choppers doesn't constitute an emergency situation. The woman said she had tried, but since it was Sunday all the plumbing companies were closed. The bedraggled operator told the woman to wait until Monday and then call the plumber, as there was no way she would dispatch an officer to help retrieve the teeth. After a brief pause the woman begged the dispatcher to send someone over. "I can't wait until Monday. My boyfriend is coming over today and he doesn't know I have false teeth."

-- 911 REPORT --

"Can you tell me if Arizona and Utah
are in the same time zone?"

A RELATIVE 911 CALL

DISPATCHER: Police emergency.

MAN: Yeah, this is Elijah. They know me down at the police station. Hey, why does that keep beeping like that?

DISPATCHER: It's on a recording.

MAN: Oh, hey, a recording, that's great. I'm being recorded?

DISPATCHER: Yes, sir.

MAN: Hey, that's great. I want everybody to hear about me. Pretty soon I'll be world famous.

DISPATCHER: That's the truth.

MAN: I'm going to Jerusalem pretty soon. God's going to take me to Israel in a spaceship. UFO. You better believe it. They're everywhere. Everybody's seen . . . millions of people have seen them all around the world.

DISPATCHER: Well, that's great.

MAN: Now that's right. God bless the police officers and the scientists and the ordinary people that talk about these UFOs. They do exist. And I know all about . . . I'm a UFOlogist, I'm the number one scientist on this planet. I'm a historian, I'm a scientist.

DISPATCHER:	Okay.
MAN:	You heard of Albert Einstein?
DISPATCHER:	No, but I'm going to have to go. I got other important—
MAN:	I can explain it to you, his theory of relativity . . .
DISPATCHER:	Well, I don't have time to hear Einstein's theory of relativity . . .
MAN:	It's very simple. E does equal MC squared.
DISPATCHER:	That's right.
MAN:	Emmanuel equals the Messiah coming the second time. It's elementary, my dear Watson [laugh]. Einstein was a Jew and I'm a Jew, and very few people in the world understood him. That's right. I'm an engineer, I'm an electrician, a plumber, anything. I can do anything.
DISPATCHER:	Well, that's wonderful.
MAN:	And I'm the world's greatest entertainer. I'm worth about fifty million dollars a year.
DISPATCHER:	I gotta go now.
MAN:	Okay, God bless you.
DISPATCHER:	Bye-bye.
MAN:	Bye-bye.

DR. DOLITTLE OR
DR. KNOWLITTLE

DISPATCHER: 911, what's the address of your emergency?

CITIZEN: There's a dead cow in the road here. It is causing a major traffic hazard.

Police responded to find a very small kitten in the road.

JUMPING INTO ACTION

Police in Toronto, Ontario, responded to a 911 call and quickly and easily apprehended two men who had burgled a house. The bungling burglars' getaway ended more abruptly than they expected and certainly not as planned. The seventeen-year-old sprained his ankle after he jumped off the porch and accidentally landed on his twenty-two-year-old partner. The partner suffered a fractured skull, broken collarbone and ribs, and a collapsed lung. The men were lying in a heap at the bottom of the porch, writhing in pain when the police arrived—thereby being punished before being sentenced.

-- 911 REPORT --

"I know this is going to sound totally stupid, but I was shopping at Shopko, and I've come to pay for my purchases and nobody is here and the doors are locked."

SHE'S ALL CHOKED UP

DISPATCHER: Police department, this call—she said she called before—she said she's choking and she's waiting for an ambulance.

POLICE: What happened there?

WOMAN: [Unintelligible] . . . open heart surgery and I'm choking on something that . . . [choking sounds]

POLICE: What are you choking on, ma'am?

WOMAN: Will you get your ass over here, I'm choking to death!

POLICE: What are you choking on, ma'am?

WOMAN: I'm choking on some tiny seeds that I swallowed last night. [choking sounds]

POLICE: Are you having pain or anything?

WOMAN: Yes, I'm throwing up but nothing comes out. I, uh . . . [choking] Will you hurry up!

GUESS WHO'S COMING TO DINNER

You never know who might crash a wedding reception—an unwanted friend, a stranger looking for free food, or in the case of one outdoor reception in Lake Tahoe, Nevada—a pack of grizzly bears. Don't mess with guests who've had a couple glasses of champagne, because these folks didn't run in fear—they started pelting the bears with pine cones. Soon, however, the guests were joined by two more bears. That's when manager Ron Elkins decided it was time to call 911. Deputies arrived and chased away the bears by firing a volley of rubber bullets at them. After the bears were gone the guests went back to enjoying the festivities and awaited the dinner. Elkins entered the kitchen and discovered another bear was about to help himself to the main course. This bear was easily frightened away after Elkins clanged some pots and pans together. "If that didn't work," Elkins said, "my fallback plan was to stick the bears with the entire tab for the wedding reception." But knowing how much these receptions can cost, I think that would be considered cruelty to animals.

-- 911 REPORT --

"I saw pawprints in the snow leading to my deck.
What should I do about it?"

A DREAM WITHIN A DREAM

DISPATCHER: 911, what's the nature of your emergency?

MALE CALLER: It's me, Paul.

DISPATCHER: Paul, what's your emergency?

MALE CALLER: I, uh, I stopped taking my medicine and I'm having that werewolf hallucination again.

DISPATCHER: Werewolf hallucination?

MALE CALLER: Yeah, the one where he's clawing at the door and pretty soon he's everywhere I look.

DISPATCHER: Okay, Paul, it's going to be all right. Is this frightening you?

MALE CALLER: No, it's a rerun.

A FRIEND IN NEED . . .

A young man called the 911 center in Huntington Beach, California, pleading with the dispatcher to help his friend. He said his friend was unconscious and lying on the floor. The dispatcher stayed on the line and transferred the call to Fire Emergency, which handles all paramedic calls. The paramedic began giving the frightened young man instructions on how to perform CPR. At one point she told the caller that in order to save the life of his friend he would have to scoop the vomit out of the victim's mouth and breathe into it. After a moment's hesitation the caller said, "No. It's okay, I think he's dead anyway." Like they say, with friends like that, who needs enemies?

-- 911 REPORT --

"The manager of the hotel yelled at me.
My self esteem has been damaged and I'm humiliated."

AN OLD SAYING

DISPATCHER: 911, where's your emergency?

OLDER WOMAN: I'm not sure I'd call it an emergency, but
                I didn't know who else to call.

DISPATCHER: What's the problem there, ma'am?

OLDER WOMAN: I've got a terrible burning.

DISPATCHER: Have you been burned, ma'am?

OLDER WOMAN: No, it's a female burning, if you know what
                I mean—in my possibility.

DISPATCHER: I'm sorry, ma'am, your what?

OLDER WOMAN: My possibility, it's burning something horrible.

DISPATCHER: Ma'am, I . . .

OLDER WOMAN: Oh, you know, [whispers] my vagina.

DISPATCHER: Oh, I wasn't sure what you were talking
                about, you kept saying "possibility."

OLDER WOMAN: That's just a nickname, dear. I don't think I'll
                ever use it again, but it's always a possibility.

IF THE EARTH IS ROCKIN', DON'T BOTHER KNOCKIN'

The Loma Prieta earthquake on October 17, 1989, generated a lot of frantic calls. Several were legitimate emergency calls, but there were a vast number of calls from people interested in simply getting information about the earthquake.

DISPATCHER: 911, what's your emergency?

MALE CALLER: How many people are dead?

DISPATCHER: Excuse me?

MALE CALLER: How many people were killed by the earthquake?

DISPATCHER: I have no idea, sir! It was very strong and covered a lot of area! We only handle Monterey County here . . .

MALE CALLER: Oh, I thought you were 911; that's what I dialed.

FEED ME, SEYMOUR!

"There's something suspicious looking in my plants," the elderly woman caller said. The dispatcher, thinking it might be a prowler, calmed the woman's fears and began asking pointed questions to get more information. The older woman explained that she wasn't talking about the bushes outside but that there were strangers in her houseplants, "shrinking from small size to tall size." Not to be cruel, but dispatchers, in a lot of instances, will play along with someone who's obviously a dime short of a dollar, giving them bogus advice to eliminate the imagined problem. The dispatcher suggested to the woman she scare the creatures out of the plants with a "household appliance." The woman became slightly angered at this suggestion and said, "I've tried that; they aren't the least bit afraid of my hair dryer!" Two policemen arrive at the woman's residence and convinced her they had frightened away the intruders and her houseplants were once again safe. Twenty minutes later she called back asking the officers return to finish the job. "He forgot one in the terrarium," she complained.

"Yeah, I'd like to report a 911."

DON'T HAVE A COW, MAN

DISPATCHER: Dispatch.

MAN: Hi, uh . . .

DISPATCHER: Can I help you?

MAN: Yeah, the guy before didn't really believe me, but I just saw a cow in the street.

DISPATCHER: [laugh]

MAN: I'm dead serious. I'm not kidding you.

DISPATCHER: No, I totally believe you. I just think it's kind of funny. Where's it at? Was it right in the middle of the street?

MAN: It was on the opposite side of the street. But it was in the street.

DISPATCHER: Okay. We will check on that.

MAN: It was a big black cow. I couldn't see it. At first I thought it was a person in the street just crossing it but then I looked again—it had four legs. Looked again, big ears.

DISPATCHER: We will . . . we will check in on it.

MAN: Okay.

DISPATCHER: Okay, thank you.

[Another call]

DISPATCHER: Dispatch.

OTHER DISPATCHER:	Moooo!
DISPATCHER:	Yeah.
OTHER DISPATCHER:	Are you dispatching somebody on this?
DISPATCHER:	They're going. He said you didn't believe him.
OTHER DISPATCHER:	No, I didn't believe him. Is there any place in the city that has cows?
DISPATCHER:	Don't know . . .
OTHER DISPATCHER:	Okay . . .
DISPATCHER:	Bye.
OTHER DISPATCHER:	Bye.

[Dispatcher calls officer]

DISPATCHER:	63 Alpha 905 stray and the Cedar . . .
OFFICER:	A large . . .

[Mooing in the background]

DISPATCHER:	A large black cow in the street. The RP is at 13192 Cedar. Cut the mooing.
OFFICER:	We found the cow.
OTHER OFFICER:	The cow is running southbound toward Bastille.
ANOTHER OFFICER:	I got a rope and harness in the back of my truck. If worse comes to worse I can go get it.
OTHER OFFICER:	Can you ride it back to the station?

ANOTHER OFFICER:	It just walked into a fenced-in front yard, so it's contained.
NEW OFFICER:	The cow jumped the fence. It's westbound toward Bastille going to West Lawn.
DISPATCHER:	42 Bravo.
OTHER DISPATCHER:	42 Bravo.
DISPATCHER:	He's off and running. Westbound, eastbound, Stayom.
OTHER OFFICER:	Maybe if somebody hums the theme to *Rawhide* it'll stop.
FOURTH OFFICER:	You're so funny, come over here and try to catch it.
FIRST OFFICER:	You can't really set up a perimeter 'cause that thing charges at you, so it's kind of hard to stop it.
DISPATCHER:	10-4 Bravo.
DISPATCHER:	42 Bravo. Can you ask the owner if it's a meat cow or a milk cow?
OTHER DISPATCHER:	A what cow?
SECOND OFFICER:	56 for info. It just runs around our cars, so it's kind of hard to keep it contained as you guys can see.
FOURTH OFFICER:	41 Charlie to 40, he just ran over our cars.
OFFICER:	41 we got him in the front yard with a gate on Chestnut—13731.
DISPATCHER:	Well, tell the owner and they'll be over to collect their prize.

THE THONG SHOW

"There's a woman over here doing some yard work in one of those thong bikinis," said an older male caller. It piqued the male dispatcher's interest but it still didn't qualify as an emergency life-or-death situation. The dispatcher, in a professional manner, asked the man, "Sir, 911 is an emergency number. What do you expect the police to do about a woman in a thong bikini?" The old man, without missing a beat, responded, "Nothing, just thought you fellows would like to know." Now that's a concerned citizen for you.

"If I lose my memory, how will I know?"

PUTTING A CRIMP
IN YOUR STYLE

DISPATCHER: 911, what's the address of your emergency?

CITIZEN: [calling from the state mental hospital] Yes, my doctor put me on a medication and it has kept me from consummating my marriage for four weeks now.

WHEN IN ROME . . .

While visiting the United States a European tourist was driving in his rental car and admiring the vastness of California. His car began to act suspiciously, and when he glanced down at the gauges he noticed the "check engine" warning light was on. He pulled the car over to the side of the road and dug through the glove box looking for the rental manual. He flipped through the pages and found the "troubleshooting" section, which stated that when the "check engine" light is illuminated to stop the car and call the emergency number for assistance— meaning the number on the rental policy. He went to a pay phone and saw where it said "For emergency assistance, call 911," so he did. The operator on duty sent him a wrecker.

-- 911 REPORT --

"Yes, can you send the animal shelter over to my house?"

A HOUSE CALL

Saturday, February 21, 1998. Officers arrived at a Coventry Township, Ohio, home after a 911 call was made from the house. No one responded to their knocking and they became suspicious. One officer looked in a window and saw the telephone was off the hook. They tried the door and found it to be unlocked, so they entered the premises. While checking through the house to see if anyone was in danger the officers came across a large amount of marijuana—about forty pounds' worth. When the owner, Dean A. Harris, arrived back at home he was promptly arrested. Police were busy reading Harris his rights when his pager continued to go off. The number of the display was recognized by one of the officers as being from a local motel. It was at the motel that police arrested another suspect, Anthony A. Parra. Police confiscated the marijuana, worth about $52,000, and $19,000 in cash. Who or why the emergency 911 number was called, no one knows.

911 REPORT ... 911 REPORT ... 911 REPORT
911 REPORT ... 911 REPORT ... 911 RE
... 911 REPORT ... 911 REPORT ...
911 REPORT ... 911 REPORT ... 911 RE
PORT ... 911 REPORT ... 911 REPORT
911 REPORT ... 911 REPORT ... 911 RE
PORT ... 911 REPORT ... 911 REPORT
911 REPORT

"What are you wearing?"

PORT ... 911 REPORT ... 911 REPORT
911 REPORT ... 911 REPORT ... 911 RE
PORT ... 911 REPORT ... 911 REPORT
911 REPORT ... 911 REPORT ... 911 RE
PORT ... 911 REPORT ... 911 REPORT
911 REPORT ... 911 REPORT ... 911 RE
PORT ... 911 REPORT ... 911 REPORT

AN ALARMING CALL

DISPATCHER: 911, may I help you?

MAN: Yeah, no problem. My central station alarm company called you thirty-five minutes ago.

DISPATCHER: Uh-huh.

MAN: And I called twenty minutes ago and, uh, my partner got down to our store ten minutes after the alarm was called in and no policeman showed up even though he did discover it was a false alarm.

OTHER MAN: (^#$@& your alarm.

MAN: I beg your pardon?

OTHER MAN: ^%#&^! your alarm.

MAN: Who's this?

OTHER MAN: This is the police department. &^#*@ . . .

DISPATCHER: *Wrong!*

OTHER MAN: Check your alarm.

DISPATCHER: Hey, that isn't . . . Hey that isn't the police department saying that.

MAN: Wow.

DISPATCHER: I didn't know who that was.

MAN: Wow.

DISPATCHER: I was just as surprised as you.

MAN: Wow, that was really strange.

DISPATCHER: I don't know where that came from.

MAN: Neither do I. You should . . . hold on a second. [To someone in the room] You should have heard what was going on on the phone. Somebody cut in on the line and was saying "&^#*# your alarm." That's bizarre.

DISPATCHER: It sure is.

MAN: Wow. You have that on tape, I assume?

DISPATCHER: Yes, it is on tape.

MAN: I wonder if that can be traced. I doubt it—too short.

OTHER MAN: *^#^$ you!

MAN: Who's this?

OTHER MAN: You're a punk, you. Check your own &*#^ing alarm, don't be wasting the taxpayer's money.

MAN: Hey, you wanna take it on?

DISPATCHER: Stay on the line.

MAN: Tell me who you are, man?

OTHER MAN: Go kiss my ass, you punk!

MAN: Hey, tell me who you are. We'll take . . .

OTHER MAN: &*^$#^ you, you ass*#^! Go check your own
            alarm.

MAN: Hey, who are you, man?

OTHER MAN: You call at taxpayer's money. Up the ass. Go
            check your own &#&%. Get your own security
            alarm, uh, guard over there and check your own
            &#%^&^ing business.

MAN: Come on, man, I'll take you on. What's your
            name? [Someone clicks in on the line]

POLICE: Who's this?

MAN: Hello?

POLICE: Hello, this is the police department.

MAN: Wow, hello?

POLICE: Yeah, what can I do for you?

MAN: I was just speaking to a lady and . . .

DISPATCHER: Yeah, I'm still here. This other guy comes on the
            phone and saying all this stuff and saying *he's*
            the police department.

POLICE: Uh, well, he's not, we are! Okay?

DISPATCHER: I don't know where that's coming from.

MAN: She is, too.

POLICE: Yeah, she's, uh . . .

DISPATCHER: Yeah . . .

POLICE: She's with the police department, too, sir.

MAN: Well, who's on the line?

POLICE: Uh, we can't tell you. I don't know.

[Nervous laughter from all]

MAN: This is really strange.

POLICE: Yeah, well . . .

DISPATCHER: He's done it twice . . .

POLICE: Wires got crossed, or something. I don't know.

MAN: Well, okay. My central station called in an alarm thirty-five minutes ago, now forty minutes ago . . .

POLICE: Uh-huh?

MAN: Uh, my partner got down there ten minutes later, no police have showed up.

POLICE: Okay.

DISPATCHER: I'll take care of it now.

MAN:	He did discover it was a . . .
POLICE:	Uh, sir . . .
MAN:	. . . false alarm. But, you know . . .
POLICE:	Uh, sir . . .
MAN:	. . . if it was the real thing, I'm kind of worried.
POLICE:	Uh, can you hang on? This gal will handle it from here, okay?
MAN:	Okay.
DISPATCHER:	All right, thank you.
POLICE:	Okay.
MAN:	Boy, is that strange.
DISPATCHER:	Yeah, it really is strange. I don't know what the cause of that is.
MAN:	I bet it's the weather. It's probably what set our alarm off, also.
DISPATCHER:	Yeah, but, geez! [laughter] Okay, let me check for the call.
MAN:	All right. My partner did discover, definitely, it is a false alarm but I'm kind of worried why nobody was called on it.
DISPATCHER:	Right. That sounds unusual, too.
MAN:	Yeah.

[Clicking on the line]

DISPATCHER: Is that him on there again?

MAN: I don't know.

OLDER WOMAN: What is it? Police department?

MAN: Boy, this line must be really crossed.

DISPATCHER: It must be.

OLDER WOMAN: Not the police department?

DISPATCHER: This is the police department.

OLDER WOMAN: I have fourteen units and one of my [unintelligible] said there's a man outside her window.

DISPATCHER: Okay, we'll send somebody out.

OLDER WOMAN: I've had a hip operation and I can't go down. I'm in bed.

DISPATCHER: Okay, you stay where you are. I'll send the police out there.

OLDER WOMAN: I'd appreciate it right now, dear.

DISPATCHER: Okay. Are you still there, sir?

MAN: I sure am.

DISPATCHER: I'm sorry.

MAN: No problem.

DISPATCHER: I don't know what to tell you.

MAN: Hey, we'll all go to GTE tomorrow and raise hell.

DISPATCHER: I guess so.

[Clicking on the line]

DISPATCHER: They say it's possibly a bad alarm. Is it . . .

MAN: Right. They just finished installing it today, as a matter of fact.

[The same Other Man as before comes on the line]

OTHER MAN: &#^& your alarm, you old ass&#%. @#^& your alarm!

DISPATCHER: [whispering] He's here again.

MAN: Wow.

DISPATCHER: I don't know.

MAN: Well, I wish you a lot of luck.

DISPATCHER: Okay.

MAN: Thanks very much for the help.

DISPATCHER: Okay.

MAN: Okay, take care now.

DISPATCHER: Uh-huh.

MAN: Bye-bye.

DISPATCHER: Bye.

OTHER MAN: &#^^ your alarm!

PRIMARY AND SECONDARY SMOKE

According to a story in the *Carolina Morning News*, Beaufort County 911 Center Assistant Supervisor Alexa Paugh received a call from a man who told her he felt woozy. When Paugh asked if the man wanted an ambulance he said, "No. I just wanted you to know." He went on to tell the dispatcher he had been smoking marijuana all day and promptly hung up the phone. A few moments later her line rang, and it was the same caller. "He called back and said, 'I think I might have set my house on fire," Paugh said. "I asked him if he saw flames and he said yes."

She instructed the altered-consciousness caller to leave his house as quickly as possible. She then called the fire department, giving them the information about the possible fire. The possible fire was in fact an actual fire and was verified when the man's neighbor called saying he was watching "thirty-foot flames" coming from the house. The neighbor said he never saw the owner of the house leave, and as soon as Paugh disconnected the line the stoned man called back. "He called again and said, 'I'm pretty sure now I set my house on fire,'" Paugh remembered. "I said, 'Sir, get out of your house now!'" In three minutes the firefighters arrived on the scene but the house had already burned to the ground. The house was toast, and the owner was still toasted, but no one was injured.

911 REPORT . . . 911 REPORT . . . 911 RE
. 911 REPORT . . . 911 REPORT . . . 91
ORT . . . 911 REPORT . . . 911 REPORT
. 911 REPORT . . . 911 REPORT . . . 91
REPORT . . . 911 REPORT . . . 911 RE
. 911 REPORT . . . 911 REPORT . . . 91
REPORT . . . 911 REPORT . . . 911 RE

"How do I make a collect call?"

. 911 REPORT . . . 911 REPORT . . . 91
REPORT . . . 911 REPORT . . . 911 RE
. 911 REPORT . . . 911 REPORT . . . 91
REPORT . . . 911 REPORT . . . 911 RE
. 911 REPORT . . . 911 REPORT . . . 91
REPORT . . . 911 REPORT . . . 911 RE
. 911 REPORT . . . 911 REPORT . . . 91
REPORT . . . 911 REPORT . . . 911 RE

HUNT AND PECK

DISPATCHER: 911, what's the address of your emergency?

CITIZEN: I need an officer to come out here for a disturbance. My brother is typing too loud and I need an officer to tell him to go to bed. He's twenty-three.

BOUQUET BUFFET

DISPATCHER: Hello.

WOMAN: Hello?

DISPATCHER: How can we help you?

WOMAN: Hi, we have this gentleman in our shop who's kind of schizo maybe. He's walking through here eating hair color, putting it on his face. He won't leave. We have a children's shop here.

DISPATCHER: What does he look like?

WOMAN: He is very scruffy. Full beard. He's got a backpack on him. A blue long-sleeved T-shirt, green long pants. Now he's eating earrings—the second one today.

DISPATCHER: Okay, where are all the kids at?

WOMAN: Oh, we've got a couple in the chairs. A couple of adults in the chairs. There's nobody in the waiting room at the moment.

DISPATCHER: Okay, we'll get somebody out there.

WOMAN: Thank you very much.

DISPATCHER: All right, bye.

WOMAN: Bye. [To someone in the shop] They're on their way.

JUST ALONG FOR THE RIDE

Christopher Burgess of Bullskin Township, Pennsylvania, wanted to visit his girlfriend at the local hospital. He didn't have a car and when he checked his pockets he realized he didn't have enough money for a cab, either. He thought he would be clever and call 911, claiming to be deathly ill. He did just that, and when the paramedics arrived he demanded to be taken to the hospital. As soon as the ambulance pulled up at the emergency entrance, Burgess let himself out of the back, ran through the emergency door entrance, and headed for the bank of elevators. The paramedics called the cops, who waited until Burgess came back down. (I wonder if he expected the ambulance to give him a lift home.) He was promptly arrested and charged with failure to pay the ambulance bill of three hundred dollars. If the fare for the ambulance was three hundred dollars, I'm curious what kind of tip the paramedics would expect.

-- 911 REPORT --

"The neighbor's kid punched my kid.
I want a cop to come over and arrest that brat!"

A CALLER WITH A BAD CONNECTION

DISPATCHER: 911 emergency.

WOMAN: Yes, may I speak to operator number 4?

DISPATCHER: Yeah.

WOMAN: And it's regarding my missing son.

DISPATCHER: Ma'am, this is operator 4, what can I help you with?

WOMAN: I was telling you, my son, the last time he was missing, my little sister took him somewhere for several days.

DISPATCHER: Oh. I thought you didn't know who took him last time?

WOMAN: Yes, I . . . well, I remembered just now that my sister kidnapped him for several days because she was, she suf . . . she's got a felony in kidnapping children.

DISPATCHER: Okay, ma'am. We're going to send an officer out, okay? Unless, you have an emergency . . . another emergency . . .

WOMAN: This is an emergency.

DISPATCHER: Ma'am . . .

WOMAN: [suddenly becoming hysterical] *Look!* ^&#% *you!*

DISPATCHER: Why are you yelling at me?

WOMAN: You are a bunch of &#^&! My sister kidnapped my boy [unintelligible]. You're full of ^@#%%! You're going to hear from me and the whole FBI. My husband is a CIA!

DISPATCHER: Ma'am . . .

WOMAN: His name is David James Houston Hamilton Long Boy Name!

DISPATCHER: Ma'am . . .

WOMAN: You're a bunch of &#^&! I don't give a &#%^ whether he's living or dead. You get me? I got a gun! And I'm going to use it to kill you in any emergency! Good-bye &#^@head!

DISPATCHER: Ma'am?

WOMAN: I'm going to talk to your supervisor. Your &#^^@! [unintelligible] supervisor in my pajamas. Get down here. I'm going to get out of these pajamas and blow your &#^^@# head &^@#%#!

[Call back to the 911 center from the dispatched police officer]

DISPATCHER: 911 emergency.

POLICEMAN: Is this operator number 4?

DISPATCHER: This is operator number 4.

POLICEMAN: Okay, I'm investigating a complaint . . .

DISPATCHER: Yes?

POLICEMAN: I'm sorry, what was the complaint, ma'am?

[Woman tells the officer the story]

POLICEMAN: Uh-huh . . . yes . . . you did yell at her . . . [whispering to the dispatcher] Can you hear this?

DISPATCHER: Uh-huh.

POLICEMAN: [still whispering to dispatcher] Cuckoo, cuckoo.

[Shared laughter]

POLICEMAN: [back to the caller] Oh, she said it was a bunch of &#^^ and hung up on you? Oh, you hung up on her? Okay, you said that they were possibly taking your boy and your mom, but they're here—they've been here for a while.

[to the dispatcher] Tell me if you get bored.

[back to the caller] Oh, they just got home? I'll file a complaint accordingly. Okay? Anything I like? As I just told you, is there anything you'd like done to her? Perhaps some time off?

WOMAN: To operator number 4?

POLICEMAN: Yeah, to operator number 4. We've been having
             problems with you, too, by the way. No, I don't
             think . . . no she's not . . . that will be noted. She
             also has a partner, 4-A, did she cause you any
             problem? I'll handle this appropriately.

             [Back to the dispatcher] I'm going to have to go,
             operator number 4. We'll talk about this in
             detail later.

DISPATCHER: Okay.

POLICEMAN: Good-bye.

DISPATCHER: Okay, bye-bye.

NORMAN, WHO'S AT THE DOOR?

A hang-up 911 call came into the dispatch center in Honolulu, Hawaii. Police were sent to investigate and were greeted at the door by twenty-eight-year-old Denny Usui. The police questioned the young man and then asked to see his grandmother, who they knew lived with him. He told the cops his grandmother wasn't at home. The police were insistent and soon Usui changed his story. "Oh, I think she's dead," he told the officers. "She's in the shower." And that's just where the officers found her, in the shower, "neatly covered" with a blanket. Usui then blurted out, "I don't want to say anything else until I speak to my attorney because this is a felony and I never committed a murder before." I hate to quote a movie, but "Stupid is as stupid does."

-- 911 REPORT --

"My cable's out. It's been out.
Any idea when it's going to be back on?"

A MAMMOTH MISTAKE

DISPATCHER: 911.

MAN: Hello?

DISPATCHER: 911, do you have an emergency?

MAN: Yeah, there's a little elephant.

DISPATCHER: An elephant?

MAN: Yeah. Well, no, not an elephant—a little deer.
And he's still alive over here. [long pause] Hello?

DISPATCHER: Did you hit the deer or did . . .

MAN: I didn't hit it. Somebody else hit it. I don't know
who hit it.

DISPATCHER: Okay. Okay, we'll have an officer go check the
area.

MAN: Will you please?

DISPATCHER: Okay. And it's still alive, correct?

MAN: Yeah, yeah.

DISPATCHER: Okay, we'll go check it out.

MAN: Okay, thanks. I'm waiting over here, all right?

DISPATCHER: Okay.

MAN: Okay, thanks. Bye-bye.

THE PICK-UP ARTIST

In Little Rock, Arkansas, a nineteen-year-old man, Donterio Beasley, called the emergency line because he was stranded and wanted the police to give him a ride downtown. He was told by the dispatcher that his request was against policy and that he had called an emergency number for a nonemergency situation. A few minutes later Beasley called back and told the dispatcher there was a suspicious-looking person loitering around a phone booth and gave an exact description of himself. It seemed to him to be a flawless plan; the police would pick him up because he fit the description, take him downtown for questioning, and then release him. He got most of it right, except for the releasing part—he was arrested and detained for making a false alarm.

-- 911 REPORT --

"Could you send a man over and help me get my aluminum patio cover? The wind blew it away."

FROM THE PEOPLE
WHO BROUGHT YOU "DUH"

DISPATCHER: 911, what's the address of your emergency?

CITIZEN: There is someone parked right in front of my driveway.

DISPATCHER: Can you tell me what type of vehicle it is?

CITIZEN: It's a car.

THE DISCOVERED CARD

DISPATCHER: 911, what's the address of your emergency?

CITIZEN: Can I give you my credit card number over the phone to pay on my warrant?

DISPATCHER: What's the offense?

CITIZEN: Credit card fraud . . . oh.

THE CALLER WAS BOMBED

It was a call that all communications centers dread—an anonymous call claiming a bomb had been planted at a business and was set to detonate. The caller spoke to the dispatcher, giving her all the information about the bomb—it had been placed in a bar in Hampton, Virginia. It took the caller a while to get out all the information because he seemed to the dispatcher to be a little drunk. This gave the dispatcher time to trace the call—to another bar near the establishment where the caller claimed the bomb was located. When police arrived at the bar they arrested thirty-nine-year-old Ronnie Wade Cater on charges of phoning in a false bomb threat. So why did Cater call and make a false report? He wanted to make sure enough police would be dispatched to the other bar, thereby giving him a chance to drive home completely intoxicated without fear of getting arrested.

"I've just been attacked by a six-foot-tall mosquito."

THE MACE CHASE

MAN: Hello, is this the police?

DISPATCHER: Yes.

MAN: It's an emergency. Not really a bad emergency, but let me talk to a policeman. It's going to be one pretty soon.

DISPATCHER: What's the problem?

MAN: Can I talk to you?

DISPATCHER: Yes, what's the problem?

MAN: Okay, I'm sorry, I'm all excited. My wife is an invalid. She goes back and forth through the house here. Roaring, ranting, and raving, and she's threatening me with one of those CD things. What do I do?

DISPATCHER: What's a CD thing?

MAN: I don't know. One of those squirter things you do when somebody attacks you. That's not for attack purposes, is it? You know what I mean.

DISPATCHER: You mean Mace?

MAN: Whatever it is—in the little tube.

DISPATCHER: Yeah.

MAN: Okay. Isn't that for defense?

DISPATCHER: Sure.

MAN: Okay. She has a permit to carry it. What do I do to get rid of it?

DISPATCHER: Throw it away.

MAN: Okay. Okay. Thank you.

DISPATCHER: You're welcome.

A CURLY TALE

A Thurston County, Washington, 911 emergency operator answered a call but only heard heavy breathing. It could have been a person in distress, someone without the ability to speak—or just another obscene phone call. Sheriff's Deputy Gary Daurelio was dispatched to investigate. After an extensive search of the house, Daurelio concluded that the caller was a 150-pound pig—the only occupant of the house at the time. Apparently the porker escaped from his pen in the backyard, broke in through the back door of the house, found his way into the living room, knocked the phone off the hook, and somehow managed to dial 911. I wonder if the family had plans on eating this little piggy and he called 911 to save his own life.

-- 911 REPORT --

"I was just watching TV and the news said the passes are closed. Are they?"

HER BRAIN IS RUNNING ON FUMES

DISPATCHER: 911. What is your emergency?

FEMALE CALLER: I need help. My car is broken down in traffic.

DISPATCHER: What is wrong with the car?

FEMALE CALLER: I don't know. The motor is running. I'm sitting here at the traffic light, but it won't go. I put it in Park when I stopped because I had to look for something.

DISPATCHER: So it worked a moment ago but just stopped.

FEMALE CALLER: Correct. I can't seem to get it out of Park.

DISPATCHER: Have you tried stepping on the brake when shifting the vehicle out of Park?

FEMALE CALLER: No. Ooooh. Hey. That worked. Thank you very much.

DISPATCHER: You're welcome.

911 REPORT ... 911 REPORT ... 911 REPORT
911 REPORT ... 911 REPORT ... 911 RE
... 911 REPORT ... 911 REPORT ...
911 REPORT ... 911 REPORT ... 911 RE
PORT ... 911 REPORT ... 911 REPOR
911 REPORT ... 911 REPORT ... 911 RE
PORT ... 911 REPORT ... 911 REPOR

"Hi, it's Veronica. Anything going on?"

911 REPORT ... 911 REPORT ... 911 RE
PORT ... 911 REPORT ... 911 REPOR
911 REPORT ... 911 REPORT ... 911 RE
PORT ... 911 REPORT ... 911 REPOR
911 REPORT ... 911 REPORT ... 911 RE
PORT ... 911 REPORT ... 911 REPOR
911 REPORT ... 911 REPORT ... 911 RE
PORT ... 911 REPORT ... 911 REPOR

A PLUMBER'S HELPER

Paramedics were dispatched after a woman called 911 to report her plumber had been knocked unconscious. When the ambulance arrived, and while paramedics were loading the still unconscious body of the plumber onto the stretcher, they were told the series of events. The woman had just returned from a shopping trip and was carrying in a bag of groceries when she saw a pair of legs sticking out from under the sink. Knowing they had been having trouble with the plumbing she thought her husband had decided to fix the leak himself. The woman set down the groceries and couldn't help but give her husband a friendly goose. The woman was very surprised when she realized it wasn't her husband, but a plumber. The plumber, on the other hand, was even more surprised, and when he bolted up he hit his head on the metal pipes and was knocked out. The paramedics were laughing so hard by the time the story was over they accidentally dropped the stretcher.

A GUY WITH A SHORT FUSE

DISPATCHER: 911 emergency, what are you reporting?

MAN: I'm working a booth at the fireworks thing. And we're supposed to have somebody coming by here periodically and picking up money. We haven't had anybody here for an hour and a half.

DISPATCHER: Can't imagine why you would dial 911 for that, but I'll connect you with them.

[Dispatcher calls another operator.]

DISPATCHER: I'm connecting through a worker at the fireworks who dialed 911 on his cell phone because nobody's come by to pick up money yet.

OFFICER: [in disbelief] Okay.

DISPATCHER: Okay?

OFFICER: Thank you.

DISPATCHER: You're welcome.

[The call is put through.]

DISPATCHER: Go ahead.

MAN: Here I am.

WHAT'S THE NUMBER FOR 911 AGAIN?

OFFICER: Okay.

MAN: We got a whole bunch of sheriffs around here
              and I've got way too much money in this booth
              and we haven't seen anybody in two hours.

OFFICER: What's your name?

MAN: We don't dare leave.

OFFICER: Okay, what's your name?

MAN: Can you do something?

OFFICER: Sir, what's your name, please?

MAN: I gotta go.

OFFICER: Sir!

DISPATCHER: That was pleasant, wasn't it?

OFFICER: What a lovely gentleman. What a jerk.

DISPATCHER: Whoever the guy is, somebody needs to slap him
              around.

OFFICER: Yeah, that's what I'm going to tell them. Go kick
              this guy in the knee.

DISPATCHER: Okay.

OFFICER: Okay, bye.

URINE THE WRONG PLACE, PAL

In October 1996, Thomas Springer robbed a Vienna, Virginia, bank, got into his car, and sped away with a bundle. He probably would have gotten completely away with the loot had he not decided to stop during his getaway and urinate along the side of the road. A neighbor who saw Springer spring a leak thought it was so disgusting he wrote down Springer's license-plate number and dialed 911. Police pulled Springer over for not minding his Ps and Qs and soon discovered he was also the bank robber.

-- 911 REPORT --

Male complainant—electricity is out in his neighborhood. He is making a noise complaint about neighbor's generator, which is connected to neighbor's iron lung machine.

ARREST THAT OFFICER!

DISPATCHER: 911. Hello?

MAN: Yes, a crime has been committed.

DISPATCHER: Okay, where at?

MAN: In front of my house. [gives address]

DISPATCHER: Okay, what exactly is the crime?

MAN: Parking Control Officer J. Smith had my car towed away.

DISPATCHER: That's not a crime, sir.

MAN: It is to me.

DISPATCHER: Okay.

MAN: Got a supervisor there?

DISPATCHER: Why did he have your vehicle towed away, sir?

MAN: It wasn't registered correctly.

DISPATCHER: Well, then, that's not a crime. Okay, you talk with my watch commander if you would like. If your vehicle is not registered correctly that's not a crime. He has every right to have your car towed.

CAT ALMOST GOT HIS TONGUE

911 dispatchers from all over the country have received calls about stranded cats in trees. But the call that came into the Port Angeles, Washington, communications center had a twist on the old story. The call came from thirty-nine-year-old Walter Carter, who was literally up a tree. The experienced woodsman was hiking near his property at Eagle Ridge when he heard a strange noise. "At first I thought it was a deer, but it didn't act like a deer," he said. "I tried to sneak around, then I saw it." What Carter saw was a medium-sized mountain lion. He did what any experienced woodsman would do—he ran as fast as he could and climbed the nearest tree, a ten-foot pine. "I climbed up, but it started bending over and I was hanging there upside down," Carter recalled. To discourage the cougar from climbing up after him, Carter threw his pocketknife at the cat—but he missed. He then threw his car keys, which frightened the cat into moving about forty feet away from the tree. Carter took the opportunity to head for a higher tree, but the cat followed him. This time Carter threw his coins at the cougar and climbed an even taller tree. The cat curled up near the trunk of the tall tree and was simply waiting for his lunch to get tired and climb down. But an experienced out-doorsman is always prepared, and Carter pulled out his trusty cell phone and called 911. If he had thrown the cell phone at the cougar first he wouldn't have ended up in this book—he mights have ended up inside a fat cat.

I'M NOT A DOCTOR,
BUT I PLAY ONE ON TELEVISION

DISPATCHER: 911, where is your emergency?

MALE CALLER: I think I need a paramedic. Can you send out a paramedic or do I have to call someone else?

DISPATCHER: I'll take care of that, sir. Just calm down. What seems to be the problem?

MALE CALLER: I saw a medical special on TV last night about a rare disease, and I think I have all the symptoms. My neighbor thinks I do too.

THE ITSY BITSY SPIDER

DISPATCHER: 911, what is the location of your emergency?

CITIZEN: Yes, there's a fellow here who was bit on his . . . well, his unit, and I think he needs some help. He says it was a poisonous spider of some sort. He wants me to suck out the poison, but I am not going to do that.

BUILDING A STRONG FOUNDATION

A young voice on the other end of the phone pleaded with the 911 operator in Peterborough, Ontario, to help him thwart an attempted robber. The stressed-out seven-year-old was squealing on his sister, who had stolen his special Legos. The young boy begged the operator to help him get his favorite building blocks out of the hands of his four-year-old sister. The operator allowed the baby-sitter to intervene instead of the police and the quarrel was quickly quashed. I wonder if that's why the blocks are called "Lego."

-- 911 REPORT --

"Yes, is this the place I can get the
cream that melts away fat?"

CIRCLING THE NEIGHBORHOOD

DISPATCHER: Dispatch.

WOMAN: Hi, this may sound kind of weird, but in the trees there's like thirty vultures.

DISPATCHER: Okay.

WOMAN: Isn't that weird?

DISPATCHER: Yeah. It, it's kind of unusual. But, uh, is there anything you think they're attracted to in the area?

WOMAN: Well, that's what we're thinking. What if there's something behind there? 'Cause there's, like, a lot of trees and bushes in the, in her backyard. There's a huge eucalyptus tree in there and there's, like, tons of them in there. And it's kind of creepy.

DISPATCHER: Okay, but it's directly behind her back fence, then, correct?

WOMAN: There's a lot of brush and there's kind of like a ditch.

DISPATCHER: Okay. We'll have somebody go check it out there, okay?

WOMAN: Okay.

DISPATCHER: All righty.

WOMAN: Thanks. I didn't even know that they're, like, in the wild here.

DISPATCHER: Yeah, I've never seen any out here. But are you sure that they're vultures?

WOMAN: They look just like them. You know, they're hunched like [unintelligible].

DISPATCHER: Yeah.

WOMAN: It's creepy. The only thing around me is when something that's dead or dying.

DISPATCHER: True. Okay, we'll check it out. Hopefully it's nothing.

WOMAN: Okay, thank you.

DISPATCHER: Bye-bye.

[Dispatcher receives a call from the police]

DISPATCHER: 911.

POLICE: Hey, this is sort of eerie. I'm, it's . . . they are vultures. I have never, ever seen vultures.

DISPATCHER: I haven't either.

POLICE:	It's like an Alfred Hitchcock movie. I mean, it's really weird. They're all in the trees and they're all sort of hanging out there. And when you shine your light on them their eyes get all red and glowy.
DISPATCHER:	Ohhhhhh . . . creepy.
POLICE:	And there is a big pile of brush below them that have little cubbies that you can walk through, but I am not going to walk through there by myself.
DISPATCHER:	Uh, yeah.
POLICE:	Considering what vultures do when they hang out it's worth sending another officer out here.
DISPATCHER:	Absolutely.
POLICE:	So we can go snoop around in the bushes.
DISPATCHER:	Okay.
POLICE:	Okeydoke?
DISPATCHER:	All righty. Bye.
POLICE:	Bye.

I NEED THAT LIKE I NEED
A HOLE IN THE HEAD

A construction worker in Bethlehem, Pennsylvania, was using a miter saw in the basement of another man's home when he accidentally slipped and cut off his own hand. The pain was excruciating, and twenty-five-year-old William Bartron couldn't stand it any longer. He reached to his side and pulled out a gun and shot himself in the head more than a dozen times. But he didn't die. Why not? Because he shot himself in the head with a nail gun. The man who owned the house called 911, and paramedics took Bartron to the hospital, where his hand was successfully reattached. The 2.5-centimeter nails were removed from the wounded man's head and he was last reported in stable condition. I've heard of hitting the nail on the head, but . . .

-- 911 REPORT --

"I locked my keys in the car.
Can you unlock it?"

KEEP YOUR NOSE CLEAN

DISPATCHER:	911, can I help you?
OLDER MAN:	Yeah, I need a paramedic.
DISPATCHER:	Let me transfer you.
FIRE DEPARTMENT:	Fire Emergency. Fire Department?
DISPATCHER:	Fire, I had a male calling for paramedics. I don't know if he hung up or not.
OLDER MAN:	Hello? Yeah, I need a paramedic.
FIRE DEPARTMENT:	Where at?
OLDER MAN:	Hello?
FIRE DEPARTMENT:	Where at?
OLDER MAN:	Yeah. What's wrong?
FIRE DEPARTMENT:	What's the address?
OLDER MAN:	1576 Longwood Boulevard Space 142.
FIRE DEPARTMENT:	Is that the Beachwood?
OLDER MAN:	Huh?
FIRE DEPARTMENT:	Beachwood?
OLDER MAN:	What?
FIRE DEPARTMENT:	Are you at the Beachwood Mobile Park?
OLDER MAN:	It's a mobile home.

FIRE DEPARTMENT:	What's wrong?
OLDER MAN:	142.
FIRE DEPARTMENT:	What's wrong?
OLDER MAN:	What?
FIRE DEPARTMENT:	What's wrong?
OLDER MAN:	What's wrong?
FIRE DEPARTMENT:	Yeah, what's wrong?
OLDER MAN:	Uh, my wife, she's got a nosebleed.
FIRE DEPARTMENT:	Uh-huh.
OLDER MAN:	She's in the tub and it's bleeding quite a bit.
FIRE DEPARTMENT:	Is that the only thing wrong with her?
OLDER MAN:	Yeah.
FIRE DEPARTMENT:	Okay, I want you to have her lean forward and pinch her nose.
MAN:	Pinch her nose?
FIRE DEPARTMENT:	Yeah. Are you in the same room with her?
OLDER MAN:	Okay, I'll pinch her nose.
FIRE DEPARTMENT:	Sir? Sir? Hello?
[Woman screams in the background]	
OLDER MAN:	Hello? Are they coming?
FIRE DEPARTMENT:	Yes, they're on their way.

THAT SURE LOOKS LIKE A SHRIVELED-UP WEED TO ME!

It was a warm summer's night in Pleasant Gap, Pennsylvania, when Pam Watkins and her fifteen-year-old daughter looked out the window to see their neighbor doing yard work. Not such an odd occurrence in the suburbs except for one thing (or actually, the lack of one thing)—clothes. Sixty-two-year-old Charles Stitzer was going about his yard work wearing only his shoes and a watch (very fashionable, I must add). He was arrested for indecent exposure, and during his trial he told the judge he liked to garden in the nude and often mowed his lawn wearing only a thong. Stitzer said he wished his neighbor would simply dim her outdoor floodlights. Centre County Judge Charles Brown ruled that Stitzer would face incarceration the next time he was caught wearing anything less than a thong while outside. I'm sorry, but the thought of a nude sixty-two-year-old man is bad enough—but a sixty-two-year-old man in a thong . . .

SOUNDS LIKE HE'S ALREADY
TURNED INTO A PUMPKIN

DISPATCHER: 911, what is the location of your emergency?

CITIZEN: Yes, I just wanted to let you know that I have some information that will help you to solve many of your cases.

DISPATCHER: [noting that the screen indicates the call originates from to the state hospital] Okay, go ahead with that information.

CITIZEN: I am prepared to meet with the detectives and to reveal the true identity of Cinderella's stepmother.

DISPATCHER: Okay.

CELL PHONE

A call came into the Seattle, Washington, 911 center from a thirty-seven-year-old man who reported he had been shot. When police arrived, the man collapsed in front of them, saying he'd been hit by a bullet. Officers saw no blood and on further investigation found no injuries to the man whatsoever. The man, however, continued to insist he had been shot. Then he changed his story and said he had been "assaulted"; then he once again claimed he had been shot. Finally, he decided to keep his mouth shut. A witness told police the man had a history of harassing a neighbor woman and that he had recently been chased away from her residence. The man was arrested for harassment and making a false 911 report. Several hours after his arrest, a 911 call came in claiming that a three-year-old child who lived at the harassed woman's address was being neglected. Police went back to the residence and found the child in perfect health. It was soon discovered the phone call had originated from jail! You've got to really be angry with someone when you use your one phone call like that.

911 REPORT . . . 911 REPORT . . . 911 REPORT
. 911 REPORT . . . 911 REPORT . . . 911
RT . . . 911 REPORT . . . 911 REPORT
. 911 REPORT . . . 911 REPORT . . . 911
REPORT . . . 911 REPORT . . . 911 REP
. 911 REPORT . . . 911 REPORT . . . 911
REPORT . . . 911 REPORT . . . 911 REP

"When is my son's
flight arriving?"

REPORT . . . 911 REPORT . . . 911 REP
. 911 REPORT . . . 911 REPORT . . . 911
REPORT . . . 911 REPORT . . . 911 REP
. 911 REPORT . . . 911 REPORT . . . 911
REPORT . . . 911 REPORT . . . 911 REP
. 911 REPORT . . . 911 REPORT . . . 911
REPORT . . . 911 REPORT . . . 911 REP

HEY, WHAT'S SHAKIN'?

This call came in shortly after an earthquake shook central California.

DISPATCHER: 911, fire or emergency?

MALE CALLER: Wow, what did that one register?

DISPATCHER: Excuse me, sir?

MALE CALLER: The earthquake, it was a big one. What did it register?

DISPATCHER: I have no idea, sir. If there's no emergency please disconnect the line.

MALE CALLER: Will there be a tidal wave?

DISPATCHER: I don't think so, sir; usually tsunamis occur on the *other* side of the ocean from an earthquake.

MALE CALLER: Well, has anyone warned Japan, then?

DISPATCHER: I really don't know, sir. Thanks for the suggestion!

A SIX-PACK OF TROUBLE

A woman in Vermont called 911 claiming her husband had assaulted her. Police arrived at the residence to find the woman throwing beer bottles, a frying pan, and other objects at her cowering husband. The very intoxicated woman was subdued and through slurred speech explained the nature of the assault. She claimed her husband had refused to go to the store and buy more beer for her. He then took the car keys so she couldn't go herself. She felt his refusal was a form of personal assault and, therefore, she had made the 911 call. She then asked the police officers if they could buy her beer. When they refused, she spat on them, yelled, and kicked them. She somehow managed to pull loose from the officers and bite one of them on the leg. She was restrained again and this time she was arrested for assault and resisting arrest. Seems she was looking for more than one type of beer chaser.

911? WHAT'S THAT SPELL?

DISPATCHER: 911, fire or emergency?

WOMAN: I was wondering if you could help me spell something.

DISPATCHER: What word do you need help with?

WOMAN: *Something.*

MY FAVORITE MARTIAN

DISPATCHER: 911.

OLDER WOMAN: These people on the back of my property need to be stopped.

DISPATCHER: What people need to be stopped?

OLDER WOMAN: These people are bothering me on my property.

DISPATCHER: What people are bothering you?

OLDER WOMAN: The dealer that used to live next door that moved out.

DISPATCHER: What are they doing?

OLDER WOMAN: They want . . . you should see the size of the hole they put in the side of my foot again.

DISPATCHER: They put a hole in the side of your foot?

OLDER WOMAN: Yes, they did.

DISPATCHER: How did they do that?

OLDER WOMAN: Well, the laser beam out here. They pop electricity and laser beams all the time.

DISPATCHER: They're shooting beams at you?

OLDER WOMAN: Yes, they did. And they hit me in the ass, too!

"Can my woman refuse to let me shower with her?"

A PAIN WITH A STAIN

A frantic woman made a call into the communications center in Boise, Idaho. What was her emergency? She had spilled red nail polish on her beige carpet. The operator tried to explain the call wasn't a life-or-death situation, to which the woman gave a very typical response: "I'm a taxpayer! And I demand that you send someone out here immediately!" Needless to say the operator didn't dispatch an officer to her home. She didn't call her a carpet cleaner, either.

JOHN 9:11

DISPATCHER: 911 emergency.

WOMAN: I'd like to speak to Detective Foster or Detective Martin. Are they there?

DISPATCHER: No, they aren't.

WOMAN: Oh, I sure want them to call me.

DISPATCHER: What's the problem?

WOMAN: Nothing. I just wanted them to know that I have accepted Jesus and how wonderful it is—how things have just turned around in my life.

SOURCES

(Albany) *Knickerbocker News*

(Allentown) *The Morning Call*

Associated Press

Atlanta Journal-Constitution

(Baltimore) *The Sun*

(Boulder) *Daily Camera*

Bradenton (Florida) *Herald*

Calgary Herald

The Canadian Press

Chicago Tribune

The Cincinnati Post

Columbia State

The Columbus (Ohio) Dispatch

Columbus (Ohio) *Ledger-Enquirer*

Dayton Daily News

Denver Rocky Mountain News

Detroit Free Press

Duluth News-Tribune

The Edmonton Journal

The Evansville (Indiana) Courier

(Fort Lauderdale) *Sun-Sentinel*

The (Fort Wayne, Indiana) *News Sentinel*

The Fresno Bee

(Gary, Indiana) *Post Tribune*

Grand Forks (North Dakota) *Herald*

Greensboro (North Carolina) *News & Record*

Houston Post

Jackson (Michigan) *Citizen Patriot*

The Kentucky Post

The Knoxville News-Sentinel

The Lawrence (Kansas) *Journal-World*

Lexington Herald-Leader

(Los Angeles) *Daily News*

Los Angeles Times

The Macon (Georgia) *Telegraph*

The (Madison) *Capital Times*

The (Madison) *Wisconsin State Journal*

The Medina County (Ohio) *Gazette*

The (Memphis) *Commercial Appeal*

The Miami Herald

(Minneapolis) *Star Tribune*

The (Myrtle Beach) *Sun News*

The (New Jersey) *Record*

The (New York) *Newsday*

The New York Times

(Norfolk) *Ledger-Star*

The Orlando Sentinel

The Palm Beach Post

The (Panama City) *News Herald*

The Philadelphia Inquirer

The (Phoenix) *Arizona Republic*

Phoenix Gazette

Pittsburgh Post-Gazette

Portland (Maine) Newspapers, Inc.

Reuters

Richmond Times-Dispatch

Roanoke Times

The Sacramento Bee

St. Paul Pioneer Press

St. Louis Post-Dispatch

St. Petersburg Times

San Francisco Examiner

San Jose Mercury News

Sault Star

Seattle Post-Intelligencer

The Seattle Times

(Spokane) *Spokesman-Review*

The Tampa Tribune

UPI

USA Today

The Washington Post

The Washington Times

The York (Pennsylvania) *Daily Record*